CW00502420

The Fairy Godmother Mindf*ck

The Fairy Godmother Mindf*ck

How To Rewrite Your Life Story,
Create Your Own Destiny and
Have a Happy Ever After.

Jools Riddell

© Jools Riddell 2021

All rights reserved. No part of this publication may be reproduced, distributed, or transmitted in any form or by any means, including photocopying, recording, or other electronic or mechanical methods, without the prior written permission of the publisher, except in the case of brief quotations embodied in reviews and certain other non-commercial uses permitted by copyright law.

The advice and strategies found within may not be suitable for every situation. This work is sold with the understanding that neither the author nor the publisher are held responsible for the results accrued from the advice in this book.

www.joolsriddell.com

This book is
dedicated to my husband Gordon,
whose unwavering love and
belief in me when I had the
odd wobble got me through

Contents

Introduction

Happy Ever After?
What Does That
Mean Anyway?

WHEN I WAS A KID, I loved fairy stories. Kids getting shoved in ovens or fighting big hairy arsed wolves. Royalty holding outrageous balls every weekend. (I assume midweek was spent locking up daughters in towers or setting the most ridiculous challenges to any prince who turned up willy-nilly on your doorstep; royal diaries were pretty full back then.) Talking pigs with dubious construction skills, dragons, wicked step-parents and, best of all, fairy godmothers showing up out of nowhere to produce fuck-off dresses and mad types of transport to the biggest parties in town. What was not to love?

Disney showered us with princesses, throwing catchy songs into the mix. Cut to six-year-old me swooping around my bedroom with my Snoopy doll singing along to *Once Upon a Dream*. I read precociously early and immersed myself in *Grimm's Fairy Tales* and Hans Christian Anderson books over and over, lost in the stories and the wonderful illustrations of Rackham, Pyle, Beardsley, Robinson and the like. I would gasp at the utter

1

stupidity of kings who were meant to be wise and gracious. Fret over the trials set for the prince to save the princess. Freeze in terror at the ogre/wolf/giant about to set upon the hero and the cruelty of stepmothers and witches. Although I could see how some kids were bloody annoying and quite frankly needed shoving in an oven if they started eating your house without asking... rude! Sometimes I even felt concerned for the villain and worry about the giant losing his golden goose or the three bears having their house broken into and their stuff vandalised. But whatever the situation, I knew it would always end up with '... and they lived happily ever after'.

What the hell does that mean – 'happily ever after'? Was Cinderella happy being married and wealthy? Snow White was already a princess, so couldn't she have raised an army and kicked arse. (Have a read about the real-life Princess Matilda, she did exactly that, having escaped from Oxford Castle using knotted sheets... for real!) I always wanted the story to cover what happened next. I wanted to know if the dragon got any chums because he seemed kind of lonely; if the witch changed her ways and set up a thriving shoe shop; what Hansel and Gretel did after they escaped? What did those princesses *do* for the rest of their lives that made them so happy ever after? I always had a suspicion there was so much being kept from me, a bigger story.

Fast forward 40-odd years and working as a certified NLP coach and clinical hypnotherapist with an international clientele wanting a change of direction in their lives, I now realise the fairy-tale concept is a mind fuck! The whole damned thing isn't just a lie but dangerous too. The idea that we have a fairy godmother, someone who will just turn up when we need them and magic away our troubles? What a load of guff! How many people sit amid their shit waiting for that to happen rather than climb out themselves?

What if you were your own fairy godmother? What if you have the power or magic deep down inside to take you to the ball, whatever that ball may be, whatever the ball represents in your own life: an awesome career, abundance, love? In fact, wait a minute, what if *every* character in those fairy tales was within you? Cinderella, Sleeping Beauty, the witch, the prince, even the troll under the bridge, what if they are all a part of you and your own story? And the big what-if... what if by understanding fairy tales and the characters in them, you could combine the powers of all the characters. And that's precisely what I am going to share with you in this book because I spend my days helping people do exactly that in my clinical practice, to not only understand and believe that you have that power but how to use it to create your best life story plot ever!

In discovering your inner fairy godmother, you will see that *you* have the magic to manifest your deepest desires and live the most incredible life you always dreamed of, to write your own story, your way, your life, and that you had that power all along.

Now that's the biggest mind fuck of all, in the best possible way.

Chapter One

How Stories Take Shape in the Mind

Your Invitation to the Ball Awaits

I MET AND MARRIED SOMEONE in less than 12 months when I was 22 years old. No big ball, prince or glass slipper nonsense for me. I was reeling from losing the love of my life and said yes when my rebound relationship asked me to marry them. What did I have to lose?

Back then, I didn't realise that I could choose my own story, my own path, so I just floated along, letting life happen to me rather than taking any action or responsibility for outcomes or direction. If I were to draw a picture of me back then, it would be of sighing and shrugging my shoulders as I sat by the fan, watching the excrement fly through the air. It was a case of 'whatever, this guy wants to marry me, and I believe that I love him because I need to feel love and hell, I'm in no fit state to love myself, so let's let someone, anyone, else do it and make everything better, life shall be fine.

The bit about not loving myself was something I didn't realise on a conscious level back then, but it led to negative thoughts that, in turn, led to low self-esteem fuelled behaviours. Like eating lunch in a toilet cubicle at work rather than go to the canteen because I was sure no one would want to sit with me or allowing a boyfriend to mistreat me because I didn't deserve to be loved.

Over the years, I slowly realised, hey, I'm actually a rather nice person. Sure I have some habits that may irritate others, such as being a little messy. But maybe, just maybe, that is other people's problem, not mine and part of my creative nature, just who I am. Being super tidy was an issue other folks had, not my problem, or as I learned to say, 'Not my circus, not my monkeys, sweetie!'[1]

When I say over the years, to be honest, it can be counted in decades. It took me until my thirties, a bad marriage and a messy divorce (everyone but me knew that was coming) to start looking inside myself. First by buying every self-help book going, then after a while actually reading them, followed by getting down to doing what they suggested. That bit often didn't happen until a year or two after buying the book.

Finally, now in my 50s, I flipping love my awesome self, but it doesn't have to take you so long. You have bought this book, I assume, in the hope that you can change things that you are unhappy with in your life and wish to change it, yay! The bad news is that just buying it isn't going to change anything, although I do thank you. Nope, just owning this book doesn't make it a fairy godmother type thing. There is no instant fabulous, kick-arse life happening simply because you now own it. But it *is* a start, and reading it is an even bigger start.

The good news is that if you take on board the ideas here, really absorb them and let them brew deep down in your soul, then the magic starts. The good, knicker-wetting best news is that you can start creating your own amazing story now, not in a couple of years or decades, but now. You can

---

1 Translation of a traditional Polish saying.

do this. I have your back and will be cheering you on all the way. Think of me as that bestie who only wants what's best for you and sees through all your bs and excuses. I know those excuses and bullshit because I have been there and used them myself. I shall be your buddy who talks straight and with love, so much love. I learned to believe in myself, and I believe in you too.

You've got this.

Stories Take Shape in Your Subconscious

The stories we tell both about ourselves and other people shape our lives. Whether it is 'I am so useless with money,' 'I am such an idiot!' 'You can always rely on me to fuck everything up!' 'I couldn't possibly go for that amazing promotion. Yeah, I know my own manager put me forward, but they were just being polite. I don't have what it takes to lead a team.' Not forgetting the old classic, 'I am just not good enough.' When we tell these things to ourselves on repeat, we tell it to the world. Sometimes we don't even need to use words; our actions and posture speak for us. So we carry on letting these stories shape our past, present and future, to the bitter, dull end.

But can you change your story? Is it possible to *choose* the stories you tell, not simply accept them as just the way things are? Could you actually decide for yourself what you want your plot to be? Your starring role and the parts others play, they are all things you can determine if you wish. You can decide who gets minor roles, romantic roles, whether they get speaking parts or merely background nobodies without a credit. Hell, you can even create the awesome happy ending of your dreams if you genuinely feel-it-deep-down-to-your-knicker-gusset flipping want to.

When you look at film stars, pop stars, top businesspeople, even well-known online influencers, where they are in life hasn't happened by accident. They didn't get there by telling themselves and the world they weren't good enough or too useless to achieve anything. They have decided how they want their story to go and gone for it. Of course, they may not have looked at their entire story plot and changed everything; they may still have issues with their love lives, families or other parts of their lives. But if they could decide on one part of their story, then they can decide on all parts too. The trouble is that most of us want *others* to change our role in the plot and change our story for us, as the thought of changing ourselves can sound pretty damned scary; there are too many what-ifs and unknowns... and unknowns are the terrifying bit.

Comfort Zone – Boring!

Your subconscious hates the unknown as it doesn't have any previous info to keep you safe. That is how it is used to working, referring to past experiences and information and seeing what worked previously and repeating that action as it kept you safe and alive last time. Your subconscious tries to scare the bejeebus out of you if it can't find a past memory file to relate a new experience with and therefore doesn't know what response or action to take. It wants to make sure you don't even try a new, untested thing so you can stay safe in your comfort zone. That safe yet dull zone where nothing exciting happens, but at least it all feels warm and cosy.

But does it? Isn't it just a bit boring? I am not going to shame the subconscious for wanting to keep us safe; it does a fine job on the whole. We take in the world via our senses and experiences, storing these perceptions to help us navigate new situations. The subconscious remembers what worked before and sends messages to repeat that same action or reaction because it kept us safe or happy before, so it must work again. It does all this processing at lightning speed, which is pretty damn cool really, cheers subbie!

The trouble starts when brand new situations appear. For example, leaving a long-term relationship or changing careers. The subconscious has nothing in its memory banks to refer to, so it assumes any new situation must be dangerous. Hyper-alert is the subconscious' default setting in unknown situations because its primary role is keeping us safe and alive. That comes before everything else.

No, YOU Change!

This was useful when we lived in caves and had predators waiting to chomp down on our arses but not so useful now. I'll explain this brain programming a bit later in more detail, along with ways to reprogram or even delete old, stored info that is no longer relevant. For the moment, just know it is the subconscious safety mechanism that keeps us from putting in the change ourselves.

We would much prefer others to do that scary stuff, thank

you very much. It would be so handy if everyone in our lives changed to suit the story that we would much rather live. But life just ain't like that, I'm afraid. Unless *you* do the changing, the story stays the same. You could take any fairy-tale character and put them in a different setting with different people, and their story would pretty much be the same. Because their head space hasn't changed so they would repeat the same patterns, over and over, just in a different place, same as for the rest of us in the real world. It doesn't have to be this way for you:

You can rewrite your story.

You *can* change your self-beliefs. You *can* have the life you really want and, what's more, feel excited about stepping out of your comfort zone. I see you because I was there too, right where you are stood now. But I now know the hows, why and WTFs, and I know you've got this. I know you have inner magic. Sure, there may be little trips along the way; we all cock up at times, but that won't ever stop you because you are bloody amazing. I have had the trips, my clients have had trips, but we all learned to flip the trip, so I'll show you how to just get up again, pull up your knickers, adjust your crown and keep going.

Chapter Two

Navigating the Journey to Change Your Story

Your Guiding Characters: The Good, The Bad and The Awesome

TO HELP YOU CREATE your own extraordinary story and find your happy ever after, the tale of Cinderella will serve to guide you through the ideas and ways to look at your own story and change it. The story has all the major characters, a pretty but helpless damsel, wicked stepmothers, a handsome prince, a fairy godmother, and so on. I have even included some characters that, on the face of things, don't really appear, such as Cinderella's dad. Yet, it is their very absence that is important to acknowledge when working on our stories.

Each character has its own chapter where we shall peer closely at them, pick and prod at them and then, metaphorically, strip them bare for what they really are. We'll look at what issues come up for each character or what they represent in our own. Then I'll share the advice and practices to help you acknowledge and own that part of you and how to work with it, alter it or even, if needed, get rid of its sorry arse altogether and move on.

Even the most awful looking character has their good bits, trust me, so you'll learn how to embrace those parts that you may feel bad about and how to drop the ones keeping you back from your true fabulousness. The aim is to help you recognise these parts in yourself, *believe* you have those awesome parts and use them to make the rest of your life be the best of your life. I am not here to save you; only you can do that. The fairy godmother, Prince Charming? All major mind fucks. It was YOU all along. YOU have everything you need to not only save yourself but write your own story. And if those capital letters appear shouty, good! Because I want to shout it from the rooftops

YOU REALLY CAN DO THIS!

How Powerful Stories Generate Self-understanding

So how does identifying with fairy-tale characters and plotlines generate personal change or development? Fairy tales with their magical beings in a land long ago blah, blah, blah have been around for a long time and can be dated as far back as the first century in many cases. The tales have changed over time, according to the society and culture telling them, but they have always offered life lessons, defined roles and thrown in some subtle social manipulation for good measure.

Gender roles were specific, with female protagonists being delicate, unsullied flowers who were passive and did as they were told (except Goldilocks, the feisty, housebreaking mare!). Female antagonists are generally portrayed as ugly, wicked and bad for being the opposite. Men are shown as either running the country and making decisions or needing to be handsome and brave, dashing about saving damsels in distress, whether asked to or not.

Then some guys came along and pinned down the stories for us, such as Charles Perrault in the 17th century, followed by the old Grimm Brothers and Hans Christian Anderson. These writers tweaked things here and there, such as Perrault turning Cinderella's original fur slipper into a glass one. (Back then, a fur slipper was code for a lady's front bottom, especially with the right body part needing to fit into it. Acknowledging women had such things was horrifying back then, with some finding it pretty scary even now.)

Then came Disney. Enough said.

So when it comes to gender stereotypes of those old stories, let's just remember that those gender stereotypes were historical gumph. At the same time, the stories and characters are still relevant to understanding how those characteristics fit us all today – however we identify. This is the 21st century; sensible people have moved on, thank God, but it is helpful to understand what those old stereotypes represent and adjust them to suit you.

All of us grew up with fairy stories and folk tales. And I mean all, as every country, every tribe have told stories since the advent of language. Before that, we drew pictures or possibly even danced them out; it is intrinsically human to explain life, the universe and everything in a story. Especially if we have no idea what the hell it really is, such as the sun moving across the sky for an ancient Egyptian must be a dung beetle rolling it, right?

So let's take each character and look at the tale being told between the lines. You'll be looking at them, not as characters in a tale, but as sides of your own character, parts of your personality or self-beliefs – whether positive or negative. In doing so, you'll learn to take charge of your own personal story, recognise those sides that you hide away or are ashamed of and rewrite them so that they work for you and not against you. When you do that, you let old stories told to you as children control your present-day stories, which is like trying to use an old ZX Spectrum to do all your business. Those old stories are unlikely to be serving you. But there is still magic! It is right inside you and all around; it is life, and life is fucking magic! And if it isn't for you, then it's time to rewrite your story.

So, if you are sitting comfortably, let us begin with a recap of this classic tale of love and skulduggery.

What's in the Story

Cinderella is an all-time classic fairy tale with wicked stepmothers and nasty stepsisters, dead fathers and mothers, princes, fairy godmothers, the lot. Hell, who wouldn't want to magic up a kick-arse fancy outfit just like that?

Just in case it's been a while since you read this classic tale, here's a reminder. The story starts by telling us how some rich dude lost his wife and remarried a woman who had two daughters of her own. The dude goes and dies, and the stepmother favours her own offspring, making her stepdaughter the cleaner and calls her Cinderella due to being generally covered in soot and looking like shit. (Good job, she wasn't made to be a cook or she may have been called Mozzarella instead! Paella? OK, I'll stop.)

Cinderella's new blended family are pretty mean to her and completely wrapped up in making the world better for themselves. I guess they never really bonded as the story doesn't reveal how long the marriage lasted before the dude croaked, so I assume not long at all. The seriously hot prince in the local area (in fairy stories, every neighbourhood has a seriously hot prince or princess, they are ten a penny) has some pretty embarrassing parents who tell him not only to get married pronto but are holding a party at the weekend where he has to choose someone that night. Sheesh!

So, invites get sent to all the rich-arse women in the neighbourhood. Now that includes Cinderella, but the step mum and stepsisters are having none of it. After all, Cinderella is pretty hot herself, and quite frankly, they don't want the competition, with the step-mum wanting one of her own girls to have a chance at bettering their lot in life. So they tell Cinderella to get more shitty soot and stuff all over her while they go party. Cinderella doesn't argue; she just sulks at home, wishing she could party on down too... and poof! A bonkers arse fairy pops up, saying she is Cinderella's fairy godmother and that she shall indeed party on down. All she needs is a pumpkin and a few mice. Lots of magic ensues, and Cinderella gets a fuck-off dress, glass slippers (seriously? No Christian Louboutin?), and even a coach and horses.

Instead of questioning why the fuck this fairy godmother hasn't turned up before now, Cinderella happily pops off to dance the night away. Except it won't be the whole night because for some unexplained reason, the magic only lasts until midnight, and after that, her life will be shit again. At the ball, the prince takes one look at hot stuff Cinderella and falls head over heels in love, dancing with her the whole night. The step-mum and sisters don't recognise Cinderella when she is not covered in shit due to the spell, and I guess a Clark Kent/Superman glasses on/glasses off daft kind of thing.

Cinderella almost forgets the crappy part of the spell and realises too late that time is cracking on. The clock starts to chime midnight, and in a panic, she legs it out of there, dropping a glass slipper on the way. The prince legs it after her and finds her shoe, which he keeps in a weird, fetish sort of way. He has decided he will marry this woman he has danced with for a couple of hours or so, and not only that, but he will also go check out every woman in the neighbourhood to see if the shoe fits because, obviously, only one girl could possibly fit a shoe. Such is the thinking in these far-off magical lands. He will only know her because the shoe fits, not because he remembers what she looked like.

Off he pops with some probably pretty incredulous but hey-he-pays-us-so-whatever staff, because he can't carry the shoe himself, and knocks on every door, getting random women to try the shoe. We assume that Cinderella has underdeveloped feet as no one can squeeze their giant trotters into the glass slipper. In some stories, the stepsisters even try to cut off their toes to get the shoe on. The step mum has, of course, hidden Cinderella out of the way for this foot-fetish public trial, but she is found, and gosh-what-a-surprise the shoe fits, and he suddenly remembers what the love of his life looked like after all. All happy days and happy ever after stuff.

Distilling Meaning from Madness

The general idea of the tale is that life kicked the ladder away

20

from under a woman, who simply took it without argument. She didn't walk out of her terrible life to make a better one for herself or even tell her step mum to sod off with the whole cleaning thing because she is getting a job down Sainsbury's. No, she has so little self-belief and self-confidence that she accepts this is her life now. In fact, when her fairy godmother shows up and says she can magic up any amazing, good stuff, the good stuff to Cinderella is simply having a night off and going to a big party. Not 'Get shot of my step-mum and sisters and make me CEO of my own company.' Indeed, Cinderella doesn't even question why the hell this fairy godmother only decided to turn up now!

The social moral of the original story was whatever your lot in life as a woman, as long as you are pretty and demure, you'll be fine in the end because someone will come along and save you. But if you are determined to go after your own goals in life, putting your needs before others and being a bit of a sod about it, you are ugly and bad with a sorry ending coming your way. For guys, the moral seems to be that if you are young, then do as your authority figures say, no matter how bonkers or how much it goes against your own wants and needs. Plus, women will fall instantly in love with you after a couple of dances. Be dashing and full of much derring-do, never cry and never ever say you really would rather not, thank you very much. If you are an older bloke, you are bound to be king and make decisions for others – sensible or not. Your kingdom, your rules. And if you are a queen? Just go along with your husband, dear.

Could any of these characters have rewritten their story? Are we destined to just play out a predetermined role in life?

Obviously, the answer you are hoping for is no. Otherwise, why read this book. But why do we act out the same old stories day after day, year after year? It's not like we are actually born with those set patterns. We are all born naked physically and metaphorically, just blank canvases on entry into this crazy, beautiful life. Sure, there is what I call the fanny lottery, as in you don't get to choose whose fanny you emerge from, where that fanny is geographically, your ethnicity or culture, eyes or hair. That is all down to the birth lottery. If we got to choose, we would all choose a super-rich, entitled fanny, where we fell out onto silken sheets with a silver spoon shoved immediately in our gobs by adoring, loving parents, wouldn't we? A life where things came to us easily and great opportunities showed up at our fingertips. But life ain't like that for most of us. So we emerge wherever and from whomever, not even knowing those wriggly limbs we see before us are our own, never mind knowing how to make fair judgements and great choices, what is good, what is bad etc. We just *are*.

A Baby's World of Abundance

As babies, we know some basics, though, like when we are hungry or tired, when we feel discomfort from being covered in our excrement or pee and not enjoying the sensation much etc. And we know to shout out about such matters. There is no worrying that the big person with the lovely squishy milk dispensers is tired because it is 3 a.m. Babies live in a world with no worries or feelings of being bad for asking. They yell when hungry, stop eating when full and sleep when tired, and never mind if it's right there in the shopping trolley in the middle of the frozen aisle just 5 minutes away from needing to go back in the car. They wake when they are done sleeping or hungry, never mind if it is 2.30 a.m.

Most kids live in a world of incredible abundance, where food arrives on demand, a lovely bearded tubby guy in a red outfit brings you whatever you ask for, and crazy arse fairy dudes leave money under your pillow for body parts you no longer need. My niece wrote out her birthday present wish list and had 'the house over the road' as one of her requests. Why not? In her mind, it might happen, or it might not, but it seemed perfectly reasonable to ask. I remember often getting whatever I had asked Father Christmas for, from a cowboy outfit to a doll that wets itself (why do kids find those dolls so fascinating?), it all just magically arrived. I now realise I was guided by my parents when writing my letter to Father Christmas by what was available in Mum's Freeman's catalogue but was blissfully ignorant of any coercion at the time.

As babies and kids, we feel free to request whatever our bodies need and our hearts require and stop naturally when we've had our fill, get tired or bored. Then people knock out that natural gift with any and more of the following: That's-Too-Expensive; We-Can't-Afford-That; Finish-What's-On-Your-Plate; There-Are-People-Without-Anything-So-Be-Grateful; I-Have-Too-Much-To-Do; I-Can't-Be-With-You-Right-Now; Stop-Being-So-Stupid; Money-Doesn't-Grow-On-Trees... The list is almost endless, and it crushes our sense of being free to ask for what we need.

It's All in Your Brain Programming

The trouble is, our brains are designed to take in information, make some sort of sense of it, then file it away for later use to keep us safe, work out what to do in unfamiliar situations, and generally help us get by. These become 'programs' that the subconscious uses to deal with future situations. As I touched on before, the subconscious automatically squirrels away information it receives through our senses (touch, taste, smell, hearing and sight) and through our thoughts and emotions, such as how a situation or thing made us feel. Chocolate made you feel happy, dad shouting made you feel scared. Put those emotions together with a thought and some repetition, and you have the birth of a subconscious program. If you feel miserable, eating chocolate will make you happy or people-please whatever the personal cost to avoid the fear of people being angry and feeling unloved.

As small kids, my younger brother and I had it drummed into us by our mum that children should be seen and not heard, especially if adults were talking. We were told this so often our brains stored it as IMPORTANT INFORMATION, which was then reinforced by our parents if we interrupted. This brain program really showed up when we were in the back of my uncle's little Morris Traveller off on a jolly family day out, and the back doors flew open. Morris Travellers were like teeny tiny estate cars, and we were effectively sitting in the boot. This was the early 1970s, so other than a few public information films telling us not to play in discarded fridges, fly kites near pylons or shove fireworks in our pockets, everyone was generally left to their own decisions on what was safe and what wasn't. None of the public information programmes covered what to do if clinging on for dear life to a bag of soggy old cheese sandwiches and packets of Hula Hoops your mum classed as a picnic and now the only thing between you and certain death. Nope, back then, it was fine to just dump the kids in the back of the car with the shopping and spare tyre; *they'll be fine.* I even remember the central armrest in the front of my grandad's Hillman Avenger being classed a much-coveted spare seat that gave the occupier great status and worthy of fighting over as far as we were concerned. But I digress, there we were clinging on for dear life yet keeping quiet as the grown-ups were talking and our brains remembered the IMPORTANT INFORMATION of not interrupting. So we didn't. We waited for a pause before casually mentioning our current situation, which, thankfully, our parents then rectified.

It took a long time to sort out my old mental programming of not interrupting people. Even as an adult, I wouldn't join in other people's conversations but wait patiently for them to finish. Even if I had some really juicy point to add, I would simply tell it to myself in my head, assuming they would be cross if I threw it into their mix. I don't mean strangers in the street conversations; obviously, that would be weird (although I confess to doing it on occasion, mainly in club toilets where all women are new besties briefly. I even had one new club toilet bestie insist that I feel her new boob job as she was so proud of them), but with friends or at parties where the whole point is to be sociable and join in, I found it impossible to simply join in.

Most of our programs are created between the ages of zero and eight years to get us survival ready and able to deal with any shit the world may throw our way so we can grow safely and reproduce. More than anything, nature loves to see more and more of itself, so every living thing makes increasing its numbers the number-one priority. All this makes it look like the subconscious can be a bit shit, but as I said before, it is amazing! According to neuroscientists Dr Jeffrey Fannin and Dr Bruce Lipton,[2] the subconscious goes about operating 95 per cent of your daily life without the need for you to think about it at all. Tasks like maintaining body temperature, scanning for intruders such as viruses and then sending out white cell troops, regulating heartbeat, blood circulation, digestion, hormones. Hell, it even stops you pooping yourself as you sleep (hopefully).

We don't have to concentrate on all those things because our subconscious is on it even when the conscious brain falls asleep. It also stores memories, as I said before, so it can use them to keep you safe and alive. When you walk down the street, your subconscious is taking everything in and comparing it to past information at lightning speed so you can act and make decisions that keep you alive. You see a cat in the street, for example, and memories and information are gone through as to whether it is life-threatening or not. It will probably come up with happy thoughts of bundles of purring fluff, but for some people, perhaps scratched by

2 Szegedy-Maszak, M. (28 February 2005). 'The Secret Mind – How Your Unconscious Really Shapes Your Decisions'. U.S. News & World Report. Retrieved from https://hypnosis.edu/articles/secret-mind

a shithead cat as a small kid, they may cross the road to avoid it because the brain sent a message that these things hurt and are dangerous. They may not even remember the original incident, but their subconscious does and uses that information to avoid the danger, whilst looking both ways as they cross the road because it also has information stored from adults telling you to watch out for cars as they can kill you. (Or if you're as old as me, you'll remember Tufty the Squirrel, which in hindsight was a poor choice for a road safety figure as I remember seeing so many squashed squirrels in the road. Or maybe the Green Cross Code man, who later turned into Darth Vader. We ungrateful kids must have driven him to the dark side.)

So you are now walking on the other side of the road when a hot guy says hi. Your subconscious scans its stored info and perhaps comes up with some childhood memories of your dad telling you are too big to sit on his lap for hugs now, which your brain stored as rejection and felt really bad, so rejection must be avoided at all costs. Your brain immediately receives this info, and you blank the guy and walk on because who wants to be rejected and hurt again?

So you see, as much as your subconscious thinks it is keeping you safe, it is not necessarily helping because the origin of the mental programs was faulty. For example, all cats will be like that one arsehole cat that scratched you, even though – to be fair – baby-you was poking a stick up its bum at the time. Or your dad feeling awkward about you sitting on his knee due to some old negative beliefs of his own and didn't need to be stored by your subconscious as 'if you show affection, it will be rejected by all and it will hurt so avoid that at all costs'. Brain programs are often old and outdated. For example, you are now old enough to know not to poke cats up the bum with a stick or sometimes people's actions are not about you but them. Sure, the looking out for cars coming when crossing roads is a keeper, but the cat one and blanking hot guys could do with a bit of a tweak. Like a computer, your subconscious programming just needs an update now and again, whether that is a quick malware check or a completely new system.

No Limits to Your Good Story

We can all write our own stories when it comes to our lives. We have the power to rewrite old brain patterns and beliefs so that they work for us instead of holding us back. We are fucking awesome and have unlimited potential. We just need to realise it and believe it, like *really* believe it, right down to our little piggy toenail, believe it. You need to believe it so much you get gusset dampening excited about all the possibilities your life holds. And that happy ever after stuff? That naturally starts to follow when you truly believe in your own flipping gorgeous self and start loving yourself. You really can have your happy-ever-after, and I share how in the last chapter.

There is no limit on when to rewrite your story either. I didn't get a good grip on it until I turned 50. Before then, I had every angst going and a lack of self-belief that was off the scale. I didn't believe myself good enough, which meant for anything, be it love, money, intelligence, anything! I saw any sign of affection or general niceness as potential love to jump on, meaning a long line of terrible relationships with people who also had self-confidence issues. I missed great work opportunities as I didn't believe I was good enough. As I said, I even used to sit and eat my lunch locked away in a toilet cubicle because I didn't believe people would want me with them.

Now I will happily stand in front of thousands and do a talk. Now I believe I can do anything if I put my mind to it, even being worth a million quid, which is my current goal. Me, who was taught the game 'hide from the rent man knocking on the door' as a small kid; me, who spent so many nights lying awake with anxiety over how to pay bills or whether today was the day the bailiffs came. That same me now has the ability and self-belief to be worth a million. That little girl whose mother gave her the certain belief that 'you never finish anything you start; you are such a butterfly brain' has now written a book. So you see, if I can, you can. I am going to show you the way. I will explain how the fairy godmother outlook on life is just one big mind fuck, and we don't need magic baby, we've got this ourselves... YOU have got this!

The Hows of You've Got This

So, how have you got this? In each chapter, after looking at the issues involved for that character, you'll find tips and techniques for how to rewrite that part of your story. You might find it helpful to keep a notebook dedicated to going' through this book. I am a real fan of keeping a journal as I have found it such a bloody brilliant way of looking at issues, ideas or problems and working through them without judgement. I come up with new ideas, work on my whys, whats, and WTFs, and it helps me discover my reasons or my real wishes. Starting a daily journaling practice changed everything for me because it helped me see things more clearly and set my life on course for what I actually wanted. Think of your journal as a safe space, a dear and trusted friend. Then, in a while from now, you'll find looking back on your old journals will show you how far you have come too and encourage you to keep going.

Afformations

I am also a big fan of affirmations. These are positive phrases your repeat to yourself or write down and post where you'll see them often. Your affirmations are unique to you and might be something like, 'I am amazing and capable of anything' and 'I am worthy'. The idea is great, but the problem is that our brains tend to see them as untrue. 'I am rich and abundant!' you write. 'Yeah, right! I know the reality of your bank account,' says your brain and just laughs. Afformations work differently. Created by Noah St John, known as 'The Millionaire Habits Coach', afformations are like affirmations but in the form of a question. The subconscious loves a question and can't help looking for an answer. Have you ever tried to recall someone's name whilst watching a film only to shout it out half an hour later? Or that frustrating sensation of something being on the tip of your tongue? That is down to the subconscious getting on the task and going through its files, looking for the answer. It can't not once a question has been asked of it. Sometimes the answer comes a bit late for the conversation you were having, but it *will* come. So putting something in the form of a life question is mighty potent stuff and putting that question in the form of something already true is the trick. As Noah St John said:

'Empowering questions unleash your ability to take action. The answers to empowering questions produce feelings of positive self-worth and ultimately lead to answers that tell the truth.' [3]

Always make your questions positive. So if you write down 'Why is it I know just what to do to bring in plenty of money?' Your brain will find empowering answers and examples it has. If you ask negative questions such as 'Why am I so poor and bad with money?' your brain will dig up those old files it has of all your insecurities and negative beliefs. See the difference? Always keep it *positive*. I keep a notebook beside my bed and write out one or two afformations six times each for whatever I need before going to sleep. Afformations might include:

- How can I be the best that I can be?
- Why do I find it easy to forgive my past and those in it and move on feeling happier and more peaceful? (This is

---

3 St John, N. (20 August 2013). 'Use Your Afformations? A New Way to Banish that Negative Self-talk'. You Can Heal Your Life. Retrieved from https://www.healyourlife.com/ use-your-afformations

a cracker; I can't recommend it enough for finding inner peace.)

- How is it that I know exactly what is needed to be done and when?

As you sleep, your subconscious goes over these questions, then, gradually, ideas come to you or, as in the case of forgiving your past, you start to feel more peaceful as your subconscious takes the question as reality and starts letting some inner things go. Afformations are explained again in the chapter on Cinderella herself along with how to work out your own personalised ones, and at the end of each further chapter will be some general examples to use, either as afformations or as journaling prompts, whichever works best for you.

Overviews and Action Plans

You'll also find a step-by-step action plan in each chapter for working through the issues raised by that character. There is nothing too complicated here, but it may involve digging a little deep so go easy. Don't worry about the odd trip along the way either; we all have them. Learn to flip the trips by telling yourself, 'It's okay,' just take a breath and go at it again. There is no timeframe, no pressures and no guilt. This is your story, your life, no one else's, so do it in your own time. Remember, I believe in you, so believe in yourself

Chapter Three

Identifying Core Beliefs and Setting Goals to Get Beyond Dreaming

Cinderella:
Developing Self-belief

ALTHOUGH CINDERELLA HAD NO CONTROL over losing her mum, her dad remarrying or her dad then dying, leaving her with her stepmother and stepsisters, she comes across as not believing she has any control over anything. Sure, we see her dreaming about stuff, but she never does anything about it.

I used to live a short train ride from London and would regularly visit Tate Modern or the Haywood Gallery and dream of having a painting up there with the Matisse's and the hot to trot Brit Artists who were hitting it big back then. But then I would head back to my little house that had no area set aside for producing art, like a serious artist, and just potter about as I had always done. I would do the odd doodle at the table when I felt like it, share it with friends on Facebook so they could tell me how talented I was before going off to my 'real' job of helping children and young people work out life in my roles as an SEN teaching assistant, arts youth worker and mentor.

I loved to casually mention to people that one of my paintings had been in The Royal Academy but tended not to add the minor detail that I'd entered a painting into the Summer Show, but it was rejected. This means I am not strictly lying by saying I had a painting in the RA; it was *in* the building, the missing detail being that it was in a cupboard somewhere in the reject pile. I now look at this and rather than think, *what a failure!* I say, "Wow! I had a go!' I watch the television program that covers the show and all the artists entering their work and fondly remember the whole escapade of travelling up with my large painting, walking along with all the other artists carrying theirs and being a part of something fabulous.

The thing is, many of those artists tried year after year after year before they finally got accepted, whereas I tried once and moved on to something else when I considered it a failure. So very me, have a little go, fail or get rejected and move on to something else because I obviously wasn't good enough. A bit like the time I saw something on the Internet about a licencing trade show at the Javits Centre in New York and booked a stall within an hour. I had no preparation, no business goal, just the dream of someone seeing my pictures and my becoming an overnight sensation. Seriously, there was me in a little booth with a couple of pictures pinned to the wall surrounded by companies who had spent tens of thousands on their displays with proper business plans and proposals. What I would have done if anyone had come up to me for enquiries, I have no idea, but as no one did, this issue never came up. It doesn't mean I didn't have a kick-arse time. (You should see the freebies you can pick up at these shows!) But in effect, it was just the most overly priced holiday, and maybe I would have had a great time in the Maldives for the same money.

My artwork was okay, and if I had put some thought and direction into it, there was every chance someone may have taken a licence on it for something. I had one woman walk by and point out one of my drawings pinned to the wall and say to her colleague, 'I can see that as a television character.' But of course, she kept walking because it was obvious I hadn't gone for that goal. I may have dreamed of it, but there was no actual self-belief in my abilities to see it through or to cope with failure/rejection.

Don't Dream It, Believe It

It's a good job J.K. Rowling didn't do a Cinderella when her first Harry Potter book was rejected. She kept going despite another 11 rejections before being published. Henry Ford, in his early business life, had five business failures, which left him broke before starting The Ford Motor Company. And Soichiro Honda got turned down for a job at The Toyota Motor Corporation and so started making motorised scooters at home for something to do.

With a true belief in yourself and telling yourself the right things, you get the gumption to get up off the floor from where it feels the world has kicked you and say, 'Nope, this is not how my story goes!'

Cinderella lets life just happen to her, rather than setting her own path, her own story, just like I did back – many of us do. Dreaming is simply not enough. Wishing is even more rubbish as that is just hoping for something. 'I wish my paintings were in Tate Modern' is just a bit worse than 'I dream of one day having a painting in Tate Modern,' but only a bit as neither includes any action or real belief in it happening. Rowling, Ford and Honda didn't just sit back and say, 'Oh well, it was a nice dream, but there you go.'

Cinderella seems to go along with the whole doing everyone's chores all day every day thing, whilst just dreaming of going to a party. Maybe if you are covered in shit all day long and being a skivvy for everyone, getting dressed up and boogying on down would seem a great dream. But is that no more than my Javits Centre adventure?

I loved the idea of being a high-flying businesswoman popping over to NYC for a weekend. Early one morning, I was on my way to the show, strutting my stuff, briefcase in hand (it contained a book, my purse and a couple of muffins stolen from the hotel breakfast table, it was all show). I popped into a coffee shop to grab a bagel and a tea. It was crazy hectic in there with people off to real work shouting their orders and staff shouting back. I panicked at all the choices and, while I would like to have taken my time choosing, felt stressed by the frenetic atmosphere. By the time I got to the cashier, all I had ordered was a plain bagel and a cup of hot tea. (Top tip for tea drinkers: if you ask for tea in the States, ask for hot tea with milk, or they give you iced black tea, a shock to those of us from across the pond.) Yet I didn't care as I just wanted to be seen as a businesswoman rather than some dippy English woman with stolen muffins in her briefcase. I was Cinderella at the ball, giving it large but with nothing to back it up. I just dreamed of going to New York City and looking the part, no idea of anything more than that, no real goal for life itself.

I had all the tools I needed to really be that businesswoman.

I had the skills and the intelligence, just like Cinderella may have had. I was simply missing a couple of important components such as a business plan, all the work needed to achieve that plan, but mostly the self-belief that I could actually do it. This is what it boils down to, for me, for Cinderella, for you, for everyone. If you don't truly believe you are capable and worthy, then you can prance around in your ballgown or with a briefcase, dreaming and wishing your heart away, but nothing will ever really happen. Cinderella dreamed of going to the ball but stayed in the kitchen scrubbing everyone's smalls whilst having those dreams. She could have sorted out a dress, had a wash and worked out how to get there. But no, she carried on in her shitty routine thinking, *'It would have been a blast to go.'*

Bear No Bear: The Amygdala

How many of us dream of a better life yet stay put where it is safe, surrounded by our snuggly comfort zone? The subconscious loves it there. It has put those self-beliefs in place about not being good enough or capable (ideas created from messages given to us throughout our lives) then tried to keep us safe by putting up a comfort zone where it knows what is happening and there is no risk.

You might think that making plans and following them through wouldn't have much impact on your survival, but the subconscious genuinely thinks you may die if you put one toe out of that self-imposed comfort zone. Bless its daft little arse. Inside your noggin are two little almond-shaped glands called the amygdala. These are part of a system in your brain designed to deal with emotions, memories and actions. It is part of a very ancient brain function and was bloody useful back in primitive human times with its basic two signals, bear/no bear. If you received evidence of danger, such as a bear, your amygdala would set everything in motion to get the fuck away from it, pumping out adrenalin and anything else needed to run like hell or maybe fight it. When your senses received no evidence of a bear, it would just sit back and let you feel safe and happy, with that sensation linked to not being about to be killed, which is always nice.

I remember an episode of *The Simpsons* where the mayor set up a bear tax after a lone bear wandered into town and had to be removed. Lisa questioned the tax, but Homer simply said, 'You don't see any bears, though, do you?' Inferring the tax must be working rather than bears weren't an everyday concern. That's the amygdala; it likes to keep you feeling happy by telling you that staying in your comfort zone must be working because, look, no bears! The trouble is, we have advanced a bit now and don't come across bears too often as we potter about doing our daily stuff. The amygdala doesn't know this, and like Homer with the bear tax, it just thinks no bears must be down to having stayed in your comfort zone rather than understand that bears are not really a thing in Springfield/your day-to-day life.

Your brain is capable of judging anything that is not comfortable or known as a possible bear threat. Add any negative self-beliefs you've gathered, and the smallest thing can be perceived as a threat. Walk an unknown route to a previously unvisited store to get that Cornetto you fancy? Are you mad? You have no idea of the possible risks, being mugged or what if they only do plain Cornettos, not the strawberry ones, which would be devastating, and we shall class that a bear threat! Create a business plan and attempt to be successful in your endeavours? For crying out loud, don't you remember that you are rubbish with money, and you will only end up penniless or homeless, looking like a fool and, well, bears!

Your brain wants to keep you safe at all costs. It may let you play a bit, let you wander down 40th Street with stolen muffins pretending you are a highflyer, but it knows that you'll just go home in a few days because this is a holiday, really, like one of those experience trips you can buy. There is no real risk. And so, we potter about in our comfort zones dreaming of more. For Cinderella, the fear of a different life must be huge. The woman has never had a job as her dad was rich, so we assume she just pottered about doing bugger all, but everything belongs to her stepmother now. Cinderella wouldn't know what the real world is like at all, so her amygdala will tell her it is full of bears and that having a roof over her head, a roof she knows well, and something to eat is safe, just do what is needed to stay that way!? I remember using the exact same toilet cubicle the entire four years I was at college because it felt familiar and safe.

How many of us work for other people's dreams and not our own? How many of us stay in bad relationships because anything else is unknown and scarier? We believe all those negative ideas given to us as children and stay in our safe zone. Yet you can make that comfort zone wider and wider. Once you work out your negative beliefs and where they came from, you can turn them around to positive ones.

If that sounds impossible, I'd like you to pause for a moment and think about all the things you used to believe and now don't, so you can see how the mind copes with understanding when something is an old belief and no longer of use. Do you still believe in Father Christmas? No, yet you remember believing, it's just that now you understand it isn't true, that your parents made the whole thing up. You can understand the concept of something you used to believe in the past being untrue now, once you recognise the untruth in other things too, just like believing in Father Christmas as a kid (and I hope to God I haven't just crushed anyone who hadn't found out that truth before now).

I used to believe that money was scarce and that I couldn't save or use money wisely. I now recognise that this is an untruth. Something I used to believe but now see the reality is the complete opposite. The old belief was something absorbed by my subconscious as it took in all the information of being told how money didn't grow on trees, how it was necessary to hide from people who needed paying because we had no money and needed to hide that fact, which my subconscious took in as needing to be ashamed of not having money as well as realising our lack. I am not blaming anyone; my parents didn't know any better and were doing their best at the time. It is always a waste of time and energy to blame anyone, as it keeps you stuck and doesn't achieve anything. Cinderella doesn't sit there blaming her dad for not giving her a better sense of herself. We all just take our worlds to be normal as kids.

No Bears Here: Bringing Your Beliefs into the Light

Spotting the limiting thoughts and beliefs that have holding you back and swapping them for positive, kick-arse ones takes a bit of soul searching and digging. As I continue saying, be gentle with yourself, take your time and trust it is worth the effort because it changes so much. I have written this book. I used to believe that I was not capable of such a thing because I was lazy with a butterfly brain that dropped a project as soon as she got bored and something else caught her eye. Then I realised that these things weren't true at all, and in fact, I had a very creative mind with no one to show me how to keep motivated and on track. I set to the task of finding out how to write a book, the steps needed, how to set up good writing habits, how to maintain my motivation by picturing the end product and visualising holding this book in my hand, seeing myself signing copies, even imagining myself standing in front of thousands of people to talk about it, and I found it all pretty enjoyable. Not a single bear in sight, not even on days where the words seemed like they needed to be torn letter by letter from me, and definitely, no bears on the days the words flowed.

Whilst writing this book, my amygdala would try and shout 'Bears!' in my ear and make me unsure that I had the skills needed or that people would laugh at the idea of me calling myself an author. But I had a goal, not a dream. I had an end game with defined steps to get there, and I now knew wishing would get me nowhere. So, whenever I noticed a part of me that was anxious, worried or stressed, I would call that part out. I would say, 'Hello overthinking Jools, come sit with me for a bit.' I would picture that anxious Jools sitting beside me and gently chat to her as if she were a worried child, telling her it was all OK and that I'd got this; she didn't need to worry anymore.

Identifying that anxious, unsure part of me and making them a separate yet acknowledged part of me eased things so much. Sure, to others, I appeared a bit odd, chatting away to myself, looking to the side of me as if someone was there and laughing and talking but who cares? It was mostly done in private anyway, as most of our bear alerts happen when we are alone with our thoughts. In understanding and recognising that it was just my amygdala looking out for me, I could then tell it to shush, that I was safe, I could handle things. Yes, maybe a little nervous, but being nervous is the same emotion as being excited, with one focussing on a possible positive outcome and the other on a possible negative outcome. The sensation in our belly is the same, and I could flip a switch to tell myself it was excitement, and it didn't mean we would be fighting off Yogi and his mates anytime soon.

Why Are You Still Sitting in the Kitchen?

Cinderella needed to check out why she was okay with doing what she was told. What were her beliefs that made it okay to accept being a skivvy when it was kind of her house and partly her money, and more importantly, her life? We get that these stories were told in a different time, where rich girls were raised purely to be married off well and to be fair, there may be one or two like that nowadays. But how many of us are Cinderella, sitting there sitting in the kitchen waiting for someone to come sort it out for us? How many of us get together with a partner hoping that this is it, this will turn everything around, my partner will make everything better, they will save us from this boring life, and we shall get to go to the ball? Or maybe we just sit amongst the ashes waiting for them to spot us and come prancing along with that slipper which will fit only us? Worse still, we wait not for a prince but for a fairy godmother to swoosh us up some instant fabulous shit with no effort on our part and all our wishes granted. BOOM! Yup, that fairy godmother will not only know what it is we want from life, but she will also make it happen instantly and cover it in glitter to boot, just for the shits and giggles.

So, we stay in our comfort zone and wait. Our 20s wander past, and still, we wait. Our 30s, 40s, 50s all wander by until it sinks in that there never was a fairy godmother. She was one big mind fuck told us as kids. But unlike the Father Christmas thing, everyone forgot to tell us she was made up. Well, sod that! I'm telling you now and in shouty capitals... SHE IS MADE UP. SHE DOESN'T EXIST! So, it's time to pull your big knickers up and get your own wand out (not a euphemism). It is time to see what other fibs you have been told over the years and start shooting them down, one by one. Then it is time to understand what is important to *you*, not to anyone else. And that is when things start changing, and you get to start writing your own story, not someone else's.

It's important to know your own personal values. Otherwise, you'll just be working for other people's, and that will never sit right, either in your gut or your heart. You know that feeling in the pit of your stomach when something feels wrong? That feeling you get that wakes you at 3 a.m., and you can't put your finger on it, but it feels a bit shit? These are signals that you are not living life to your own core values and need to work them out. When you have your core values sorted, when you understand what really matters to you – your completely non-negotiable principles –then you can make a start on working out what you want in life, a direction. Make it a goal, not a wish. You need to be able to know when you've got there, so be very clear. Cinderella just wished to go to the ball, and I guess that was clear enough to know when she could tick that goal off as being achieved. But she could have made it bigger. I mean, that was a quick and easy one, really. She could have made the dream be to become financially independent maybe, or to buy her own house and have someone clean for *her* for a change, someone she would treat nicely and actually pay. Then she could work out what she needed to accomplish that, such as how much a house would cost, what her bills would be, how much fun money she wanted, and the cost of a cleaner. With all that info, she would have a figure she needed to achieve and could then work out how to bring in the spondooleys herself. A dream that becomes a serious goal, one that has realistic, achievable landmarks she can tick off as they happen.

Deciding on and creating goals doesn't stop after the first one either. You keep creating them for as many years as you want to, from little ones such as getting that pair of amazing shoes you always dreamed of (something more practical than glass) to great big ones such as travelling the world. And if you want to cover everything in glitter as you go, this is your life, dream, and goal. You go, girl!

Must-abating with Your Core Values

Your personal core values are our fundamental beliefs, what you truly believe in, your personal principles that guide your behaviour. They act as a compass, leading you in decision making and choices. The answers to some of your biggest life questions will centre on your values, what you stand for and important, and ensure all decisions and choices honour that core value. You will know when you are not acting in line with your own values by the unease, the sleepless nights and the anxiety over decisions. Too many of us act on ought to and should-do. When you live life by other people's values, you do what you feel you should or ought. Once you understand your true values in life, you can put purpose and meaning into every action, choice and decision. As Robert Louis Stevenson once said:

To know what you prefer, instead of humbly saying Amen to what the world tells you ought to prefer, is to have kept your soul alive.'

The boy nailed it there: keeping your soul alive is what it is all about. Do things because you *must*. You must because you feel it deep down in your gusset. You must because you need to be true to yourself. You must because to do otherwise just doesn't compute. You must because this is your life – your one and only life. Yup, we all need to start MUST-ABATING! When you find your why's, everything else will just fit into place. I want to emphasise here that your must-abating needs to be all about your own musts, never anyone else's. Sometimes people sneak their own needs and musts into your head when they think you aren't looking. Always check and make sure you are must-abating for your own needs and values; it is not a shared activity!

Finding Your Core Values

The way to work out your core values is relatively easy. However, it may take some deep thought and self-exploration on your part but do take time to nail it as it will give a great foundation for the rest of the techniques in this book. Your core values will be your foundation for everything else. Your happy ever after relies on knowing where you are coming from in the first place.

For me, my number one value was authenticity. When I look at that word and ask myself what that value gives me, I feel deep down in my soul that authenticity is being me and not what people expect of me. I used to express myself visually as a teenager, dyeing my hair rainbow colours, wearing expressive outfits and generally being visually awesome. But my mum was horrified. She would make me walk behind her so that people didn't think we were together. I received the message that I needed to accept her values and possibly society at large rather than my own. As I mentioned earlier, we were taught that children were seen and not heard, with the underlying message that what I had to say was unimportant.

When I did this core value exercise many years ago, seeing the word authenticity was almost like a sucker punch to my belly. So I explored the word more, asking myself what it really meant to me, how I would feel if I had it and how I would behave if I lived to it. It felt so damned good! I realised that being authentic was to feed my very soul. I also realised that in moments of my being truly authentic, people reacted positively. They actually liked real-me more than restrained-me, and that was because people recognised my truth and responded to it. We can spot when someone is keeping a part of themselves hidden or being untruthful, and in general, it can make us back off. As soon as I started being authentic in my actions and basing decisions on that core value of being true to me and who I am, my whole life became a series of fucking awesome jumps of one fab thing to another. The following simple little exercise will do the same for you.

Exercise
Determining Your Core Values

I have listed some core values below. If you think of any that are not there, just add them to it. I find when working with clients on this that it sometimes helps to have the words on separate cards or sticky notes and shuffle them about. Once you have your top 10, whittle them down to five. Then whittle down to your top three. These are your core values. List them in priority to identify which one to have at the core of your life choices, with the other two as a backup. You don't need to chuck the rest of your top 10 in the bin, they are good to remember sometimes, but those top three are non-negotiable if you want to live to your fullest, most amazing life. Set yourself some peace and quiet; this is a no-help-required task as involving others would probably have them choosing their own values and inferring they are yours.

- authenticity
- authority
- beauty
- challenge
- competency
- curiosity
- faith
- fun
- honesty
- inner
- kindness
- learning
- meaningful
- optimism
- poise
- religion
- responsibility
- service
- success
- wealth

- achievement
- autonomy
- boldness
- citizenship
- contribution
- determination
- fame
- growth
- humour
- harmony
- knowledge
- love
- work
- peace
- popularity
- reputation
- security
- spirituality
- status
- wisdom

- adventure
- balance
- compassion
- community
- creativity
- fairness
- friendship
- happiness
- influence
- justice
- leadership
- loyalty
- openness
- pleasure
- recognition
- respect
- self-respect
- stability
- trustworthiness

Be true to yourself, and the magic starts.

If Cinders knew her core values, she could start working on what she wanted to do in life and work with those values to be true to herself so whatever she decided to do would make her happy. Working against everything you believe in only leads to stress which in turn comes out as negative behaviour in yourself and against those around you. Being able to come home satisfied and sleep well is a gift you don't need a fairy godmother for, just a small pinch effort on your part, a good handful of self-awareness and a dash of kick-your-own-arse, bibbity bobbity bloody boo. You see, once you know your core values, you don't just use them on the big life decisions, but everything else too. Your values will give you a blueprint for setting your own boundaries with relationships, whether romantic ones or just the woman in the market trying to hoist some rubbish on you. Once you know who you are deep down, the whole world imperceptibly tips on its axis just enough for your life to get a whole lot better.

Goals – Tell Me Want You Want, What You Really, Really Want

Once Cinders had worked out her core values, she could start deciding what she wanted from life and setting up some goals. Some people in life know what they want to do from the start. I have a friend who, from the age of six, wanted to be a mechanic and work on cars for the rest of his life. Now hitting 50, he has been just that his whole working life, with his own very successful garage business and around 30 odd vehicles of his own that he will do up 'one day'. This guy is the most authentic person I know, giving no shits about what people think about him and being happy with his lot in life. He knew from that young age what his life goal was, went for it and is happy with life.

I also know people in their 50s who still don't know what the hell to do with their lives. I was one of them. I could draw very well, even as a child, so everyone assumed that is what I should do, and off I trotted to art school. I spent a couple of decades doing various creative jobs such as workshops for kids, murals, community arts and arts youth work, but I merely dabbled at them all, not really finding joy in any of it. Yes, I was good, damned good, but not fulfilled. It took until I hit 50 and training as a clinical hypnotherapist and NLP coach to truly explore myself and realise art wasn't my purpose. Still, *creativity* was a tool to express it, and as what my heart truly wanted was to share knowledge with people, life knowledge, then my creativity would be a way of reaching out to others. It also dawned on me that I had been doing just that for years, sharing knowledge, and it had always brought me the most joy, yet I hadn't spotted it. As an arts youth worker, I would use creativity to explore life issues with young people as well as helping them express themselves and say what they lacked vocabulary for. I adored taking people on visits to art galleries and explaining the works and ideas in layperson's terms rather than the overly pretentious speak the art world loves so much. Seeing those people suddenly understand previously alien concepts and enjoy art on a new level made me so happy.

It is never too late to not only decide on life goals but to go for them too. As the saying goes, 'It is never too late to be what you might have been.' Vera Wang was a figure skater and journalist before getting into the fashion industry in her 40s. Susan Boyle was 47 with Asperger's Syndrome when she auditioned for *Britain's Got Talent*, showing not only that age doesn't matter but that there need be no obstacles. Julia Child published her first book, aged 50, after deciding to move on with her cooking hobby and train in France. And famously, Harland Sanders was 62 when he founded the Kentucky Fried Chicken franchise. So, no excuses, get working on your goals.

No Goal Is Too Big or Too Small

Now, if you are reading this thinking, 'But I don't have any goals, I don't have a clue what I want to do or achieve,' untwist those knickers. First, let's define goals. You don't need to be talking about biggies like becoming a millionaire or CEO of your own company, although there is nothing wrong at all with goals that big. A goal is simply something you would like to achieve. It can be anything from learning to bake the best apple crumble ever (I approve of this goal and will be happy to test results), getting into the habit of making your bed when you get up or even just putting clean pants on every day for seven days in a row. If the goal is *your* goal and not someone else's, you are good to go.

If you are still unsure of your goal, pop a shortlist of things you like and another list of things you don't like down on a bit of paper. Anything there? If you like walking, maybe you could set a distance or destination goal? If you had your present weight on your list of dislikes, maybe set a goal of dropping half a stone or simply popping one less naughty thing in your mouth a week? Again, make sure these sorts of goals are your own reasons and not for someone else, or it won't happen. So think about some smaller goals or fun ones such as learning a musical instrument that will drive the neighbours crazy or swearing in 10 different languages or something.

Exercise
Getting SMART on Your Arse

You may have already heard of the SMART principles in goal setting, and if not, luckily, I am going over them for clarity, as I am betting Cinderella had no idea what day of the week it is, let alone what a goal is and how to set a good one. SMART stands for Specific, Measurable, Achievable, Realistic and Timed, a list of things to check your goal against to ensure it is achievable and not just a bonkers-arsed idea with no real chance of happening.

Specific

Make your goal very specific. Is that apple crumble going to be the best ever crumble in your own eyes (which is very acceptable as you are awesome with awesome tastes), or is the goal to be known amongst your circle for your crumble skills, or even for your recipe to be in a book or sell the rights to it? If your goal is to be rich, simply saying you want to be rich is I a bit vague. Rich compared to your financial status now is probably your initial idea, but what is rich? Do you want to be just rich enough to have a fuck-off trip to the Bahamas each year or a nice house in the country rich? Being able to tell your boss to stick it rich? Or Jeff Bezos outrageously rich? Making your goal specific means just that, getting the specifics nailed, such as 'I would like to have enough passive income to be able to hand in my notice,' and then working out how much monthly income would enable that. Or maybe your goal is to earn £100k a year. If you decide to be a millionaire by your next big birthday, do you mean a million in the bank or net worth?

Measurable

If a goal isn't measurable, how will you know when you have achieved it? By making it specific, you know when you've kicked that goal's arse and can celebrate. It is a good idea to put in smaller measures along the way, so you can tick them off as you progress. These measurable steppingstones not only keep you going and motivated but keep you on track. If, say, your goal was to get a better job. You could write down the tasks needed, such as listing all your skills, getting a CV professionally written, creating a list of potential businesses to apply to and sending them your details. Each step could then be ticked as it gets done, showing that you are on track and moving towards your end goal. Easy measuring.

Achievable and Realistic

If your goal is to walk on the moon and you are a 47-year-old florist in Peckham, you may need to get real on your arse as to just how achievable that goal is. If your goal is to have a net worth of a million, look at where you are now, add up your assets, take away any debts from that figure and work out how far off you are. What would it take to do I? Is that achievable and realistic? With property prices as they are, some of you may be nearer than you think. And if you are way off? The last bit, Timed, may help.

Timed

Your goal needs to have a timeframe. Otherwise, it becomes a wish, and you know how I feel about wishes and fairies and shit! So, you need to add a time frame. If you are way off from that £million net worth, give yourself 20 years. If your goal is a better job, 20 years may be the time frame to work your way up through a big corporation to the CEO's office has your name on it, or you may want to make it one year, or even six months if you just want out and to start somewhere else.

A couple other important things to consider when goal-setting. First, and critically, how it will impact others. Will it have a negative impact on anyone around you? Really look at how working towards and achieving your goal will affect them. Second, double-check along the way whether the goal is still your goal and that no one else's values or needs have crept in. Yes, you need to check it won't harm anyone around you, but it shouldn't change to be their goal rather than yours.

To write this book, I had to set a goal. At first, it was simply 'I want to write a book', pretty simple. To be very honest with you, I had the vision of an international bestseller where I would be interviewed on Oprah, get invited to swanky celeb parties and other general wild fantasies. In starting to lay out my goal, I realised Oprah needed to take a back seat for a bit, probably not something she is accustomed to doing. I adore her as a role model in top goal making and achieving, so not a total back seat, but she wasn't going to write the book for me. I had what I thought was a specific goal, write a book that will help people discover their inner awesome, which I considered a great goal as goals go. I soon realised this was not specific enough. How was I going to get my message across? What the fuck was the message in the first place? Who was I telling it to? I had to get even more specific on my arse. My specifics needed to get more specific. It took me some time to nail all these questions, and that was OK.

I talk about goals being timed, but that is the very end goal. It is OK to take time in working out what the hell you want in the first place and then to understand and be clear on what it is. I spent time researching how to write a self-help book. As a qualified coach and hypnotherapist, it felt odd at first, needing to find out how to share my skills and knowledge, but this was in a whole new way, not face to face with a client or in a small group, this was a new format where I wanted to talk to thousands. Becoming aware of the skills I needed to learn was a good thing and a needed thing. I researched how you go about writing a book, how to set up decent writing practices, what makes a good self-help book and what technical skills I would need in making it a physical thing. I got seriously specific on my goal.

Making it measurable seemed easy as a word count seemed obvious until you go to second and third drafts and remove chunks of writing because it was bad and unclear, so I altered my initial measurable definitions from words to time spent writing. Always be good to yourself if you need to alter the goalposts (ooh, good pun!). If the destination stays the same, how you get there is allowed to alter now and again. I knew it was achievable because I believed I had the knowledge and ability. I knew the goal was realistic too, so I just had to set a time goal, a deadline. I set these for chapters, drafts and final manuscripts, so I could tick off each step. Booya, goal made and achieved! Sure, there were dips in the road where I stumbled a bit, detours on my time frame due to getting married and other tiny glitches, but I just got back on it and kept my eyes on the prize. The goal itself never altered; the route had the odd diversion, but the destination never changed. So, get on to your goals now, and let me know when you need a crumble tasting!

Overview and Action Plan

- Your amygdala thinks there are bears everywhere. There are not.
- Get out of your comfort zone, nothing exciting ever happens there, and THERE ARE NO BEARS outside of it.
- Find your own core life values and start living by them, not other people's values.
- Get MUST-abating!
- Dreaming and wishing will get you nowhere; SMART goals get you anywhere you want to go.

Afformations

- Why do I find it easy to forgive my past and those in it and move forward feeling happier and more peaceful? (I did this one daily for a couple of months, it was so good.)
- What can I do to believe in myself?
- What do I need to do to feel more self-confident?

Journal Prompts

- Who am I at my very core?
- What would future me, who has lived the next five years by my core life values, say to me sitting here now?
- What do I stand for?

Chapter Four

Re-evaluating Perceptions and Beliefs, and Finding Empathy

The Stepmother:
What Lies Beneath

WE GET NO BACK STORY FOR THE STEPMOTHER but, by the way she treats Cinderella, we immediately label her as wicked. To be fair, Cinders sounds like the wettest blanket in town, although making her your skivvy was maybe a bit much. This woman was somehow single with two daughters to marry Cinders' dad, so something shit happened to her, be it being widowed or having the bugger run off. I've been that single mum; it's a hard life, and you toughen up quick. What this woman chose to do was marry again to provide security for herself and her girls, little knowing this guy was going to croak pretty quick too. A local ball is to be held by the local king and queen to marry off their son. The stepmother, seeing the opportunity to better their lives, grabs her chance but leaves Cinderella out of the plans.

What's in a Name?

Being left again, I don't blame the stepmother at all for jumping on the opportunity presented to her of getting one of the girls to marry this time (she had probably had enough of doing that herself) and to a prince no less, *kerching!* That would be them sorted for life. So as far as I see it, this was a strong woman who did what she could to see her daughters were secure in life. But rather than being given negative trait titles such as bossy, demanding and manipulative, she was a born leader – assertive and a great negotiator. Seriously, women to this day get those names for character traits applauded in men, and I, for one, am fucking fed up! This is not just about women either, men with purportedly female character traits get it in the neck, too, and it is time it all stopped. It is time to drop the negative titles, see them for what they are and celebrate them in people, especially kids. Some words to exchange when it comes to kids are:

- **bossy** = natural leadership skills
- **defiant** = determined and knowing their own mind
- **demanding** = assertive and clear on their wants
- **impulsive** = bold and creative
- **liar** = future creative writer (and can be a sign of high intelligence)
- **loud** = confident and sure
- **manipulative** = natural negotiator
- **mean** = powerful
- **quiet** = thoughtful, great observational skills
- **stubborn** = persistent and knowing their own mind
- **sensitive** = caring and empathic

Now, I understand that some traits could do with tweaking. Being mean could be directed more positively, but we shouldn't instantly label others this way. When we do it to kids, we risk setting up a self-fulfilling prophecy because they grow up feeling bad about being 'bossy' and hiding their natural leadership skills – even allowing others to undermine them in relationships. Giving titles and trait names to people, like we do to the 'wicked' stepmother, is a devastating act that can affect people their whole lives, and we do it to ourselves the most.

Am I overdramatic in saying it is a devastating act? Think about it. A child accidentally drops something, and it breaks. A tired, fed-up parent says, "You are so clumsy. You're always breaking things!" That child takes in the words and files them. They have to; this is how we learn as we grow. We take in not only what we see, touch and feel, but what our carers tell us. So, the child takes in that they are clumsy and always break things. It was a throwaway comment from an exhausted adult who was stressed due to a bill that had come in, not the child's accident, but it triggered them into lashing out. That child keeps that information for their entire life, using it for all life decisions. They always had dearly wanted to become an engineer, but they are clumsy and break things, so go into a safe job, even if it is dull. When others say similar things to them, they take it without question and become OK with being put down, perhaps marrying a partner who puts them down constantly. And so, it goes on throughout their lives. So yes, I shall stand by my use of the word devastating, and we shall drop the word 'wicked' for the step mum. Sure, she has some issues to address, such as developing empathy, and I shall come to that after looking at this thing we all have of not just giving negative titles to others but in keeping and believing negative beliefs about ourselves too.

Fairy Elephant

From my earliest memory, family members commented that I had the family belly, the football under the jumper belly. I remember thinking that was just how it was. I was a part of this football belly family. I was also often called a 'fairy elephant' by my mum. She would say it in a sweet loving voice, 'My little fairy elephant.' Basically, a normal toddler then. But in my head, I was some strange potbellied, clumsy, heavy freak! I was even bought a doll called Giggles, who was potbellied with knock knees, which was pointed out to me with glee. This doll had a frozen manic grin, and when you pulled her Chucky-like outstretched arms inwards, her head rolled from side to side. She would giggle in a peculiar high pitched crazed way with her eyes bobbing from side to side too, although occasionally one would get stuck, and she would be cross-eyed for a while, adding to the whole freakishness. Obviously, I loved this nightmarish doll. I was a small kid, and she was mine, all mine, two freaks together. I look back at photos of myself as a small kid now and just see a normal child, no overly big belly or trunk and big ears. But that shit stayed with me for a long time. No more fairy elephant for me and no more wicked for the step mum.

Developing Negative Self-beliefs

We all carry some sort of negative self-belief given to us by others, most often in childhood. Some of the most common I hear in my practice are:

- 'I am terrible with money.'
- 'I am such an idiot.'
- 'I'm not good enough.'
- 'I'm not as lucky as most people.'
- 'I'm not worthy... of being loved.'

Mostly these beliefs are given to us by others. A teacher

calling you stupid or lazy (more for us oldies, when teachers were allowed to say such things, along with throwing wooden blackboard rubbers or whacking arses or knuckles) or a parent criticising your money skills. But some we tell ourselves due to our misguided views of the world. Imagine a baby on a sofa, for example. The baby crawls along the sofa until it falls off the end and hurts itself. The baby may put the wrong connections together and store the information that sofas can hurt, rather than falling can hurt. A child who needs a simple hug for comfort may go to an adult just when that adult is stressed or busy and shrugs them off. A child won't understand the adult's thinking or troubles so sees it as rejection, that they are not worthy of affection.

As soon as we pop out into the world, we trundle through life, picking up cues and lessons, and we file them away as things to not only live by but to judge the world by. We believe pretty much everything we are told by society, authority figures and peers. When a story tells us that a character is wicked or evil, we just say, 'No shit! You don't give me a reason, but OK, I'll still take that on board.' Even if that character is us. But how can we get rid of those beliefs? We sure need to, those negative beliefs we gained in childhood we have used our whole lives to navigate our world, and they haven't helped us at all. Our poor subconscious kept them and made every decision and judgement based on them, not realising most were bollocks. Our subconscious thought it was doing its best by us. Bless it. But, to re-use a phrase from earlier, that is like using an old ZX Spectrum to do your work on today. You are going to get nowhere! You need to update your operating systems.

Exercise
Word Wall

If I haven't used enough metaphors yet, here is a whole exercise based on one. Read it through first to fully get the metaphor, then have a go at it. When you come out the other side and put this together with your core values, things will really start changing for you.

1. Close your eyes and imagine the most awesome, kick-arse house. Man, it has everything: a pool, games room, one of those old-style libraries with floor to ceiling shelves and a ladder on wheels (yeah, okay, that's one of my personal fantasies), whatever you want to imagine your most fabulous house. See it all, know this house contains everything you could ever want.

2. Now, see yourself trapped in a tiny room somewhere in that house. There are no windows, just a door completely covered in bits of paper, you can't even see a handle. The ceiling and walls are covered in these pieces of paper too.

3. As you look more closely, you see that on all these pieces of paper are things that have been told to you throughout your life, and you have come to believe. Maybe you see, 'You're terrible with money,' or 'I can't do relationships.'

4. What else can you read on those bits of paper? 'I'm too old/young for/to...' 'Exercise is so boring?' Walk around the room and read them all, and as you read them, see if you can see a name attached to it, the person or place

it came from. Was it your mum that said you weren't the academic type? Maybe an old teacher dismissed something you drew, and there it is on this wall, along with the comment they made. Some may be notes to yourself after something didn't go as well as you had hoped or you were disappointed somehow.

5. Take your time to look around and see all that is written and understand these beliefs are keeping you stuck in this room, unable to enjoy the rest of the awesome house. Dig deep and be brave to face it all. After all, here in this room, they are all just scribbles, and you are starting to realise they are not true.

6. When you have gone around the room, reading them all, take your notebook or a piece of paper and list them down.

7. You were probably aware of many of them, but some others may have been dragged up from long-forgotten times. Except your subconscious has remembered them all. You have a list of seriously old computer system commands that were coded into your brain mistakenly. Whoever gave you that info was wrong, either through their own faulty coding from childhood or unintentionally given by them due to being tired, fed up or whatever. The important bit to grasp is it is wrong and needs reprogramming and updating. You can now start to see the bigger picture.

8. Then remember and mentally process the positives, all those times when you proved the negatives wrong but forgot to put them into your equation for what you

believe. Dad told you how bad with money you are? Hell, you were five years old and wanted to spend all your money on sherbet-like any normal five-year-old. Still, when you think about it, he was probably focussing on saving being of utmost importance because that was what your granny and grandpa were like and what he must have had instilled in him as a kid. Actually, now you think about it, you have made some great financial decisions and doing okay, so maybe it's time to drop that negative belief taken in by five-year-old sherbet-loving you.

The Negative Nincompoop Brain

I used to think of myself as clumsy and stupid. As a kid, I have many memories of sitting on the worktop with a hanky tied around a scuffed knee or bandages and plasters. My parents were quite squeamish, something I have inherited, so it was often a grandmother doing the first aid, and I could mentally add that my frequent falls upset my parents. I was always told when running around or walking on top of small walls (a passion for all kids for some reason), 'Be careful, you'll hurt yourself. You know how clumsy you are. You'll fall!' I was forever in the school office being doused in diluted disinfectant and bandaged. I took it all on board and processed the information that I was clumsy, and it made my parents upset, school receptionists sigh, and that no one picked me for their team in PE at school until I was the last option.

My brain took all this in, along with the fairy elephant names and put it in the 'bad' file as something to feel shame

69

for. This label forgot to take notice of the fact I could thrash everyone at the 100-yard dash, even if my reason was getting it over with quickly and get back to happily just watching everyone else do their thing; that reason bloody worked! It also forgot that I could jump a hurdle due to my poor sitting posture being the same as needing to jump, with my lower legs at right angles to my thighs, like a frog.

Nope, my brain just took in the shit stuff. Our brains are good at that; it's the old amygdala/caveman brain at work again (see Chapter 3, page 33). For our ancestors, taking in negatives like predators (yup, we're back to bears), disease or injury was a matter of life or death. Even the need to be accepted by the tribe was all about safety as you were more likely to be able to fight a bear with your mates Ugg and Ogg with you, or hunt down that woolly mammoth as a team and live on steaks for a month rather than those shit berries you could pick all by yourself. The nice stuff was all well and, well, nice, such as pleasure and fun and dancing like a loon around the campfire after downing some fermented fruit, but it was aware of the negative stuff that kept you alive to do all that. Our brains are wired to take in the bad shit and do anything to avoid it before we pursue the good stuff. In fact, we are so programmed to notice the bad stuff that our perceptions are altered, and we forget to take in the positives in our thinking processes.

If I had just taken in how good I was at sprinting, then I may have put myself in for running events and been puzzled at why I was in an ambulance 10 minutes into trying to run a marathon. No, you need to simply recognise what the brain is trying to do, understand that it comes from a sense of safety but that it is flawed, you *are* safe. And…

There are no fucking bears!

If you want to delve more deeply into this topic, check out psychologists Arien Mack and Irvin Rock,[4] who pioneered the concept of inattentional blindness or the original, world-famous awareness test video from Daniel Simons and Christopher Chabris of counting basketball passes[5] and Dr Rick Hanson, whose book, *Hardwiring Happiness*,[6] looks at negativity bias. Not that focusing solely on the positive will work either, which brings me on to the next exercise.

Exercise
Clearing Out the Old to Make Way for the New

Now you can see where these beliefs came from now, and who gave them to you, you can begin making them old ideas. Bunging them in the brain file that contains gems such as believing in Father Christmas, the tooth fairy and thinking you have a future as Mrs Captain Scarlet.

Take each negative belief and rewrite it as a positive statement. For example, if you have 'I am terrible with

---

4 Mack, A., & Rock, I. (1998). *Inattentional Blindness*. Cambridge, MA: MIT Press.

5 Simons, D. and Chabris, C. (10 March 2010). 'Selective Attention Test'. Retrieved from https://www.youtube.com/watch?v=vJG698U2Mvo

6 Hanson, R. (2014). *Hardwiring Happiness: How to Reshape Your Brain and Your Life*. London. Rider.

money, write 'I can make great financial decisions.' These new positive statements can now be the start of your own, more personally tailored, afformations (see Chapter 2, page 13) to get them really sinking into the old subconscious. Simply turn them into a question by adding

- Why do I find it so easy to... e.g., *believe in myself*?
- How can/do I... e.g., achieve anything I want to achieve in my life?
- What do I need to do to... e.g., feel more confident in everything that I do?
- Why do I find it so easy to... e.g., believe that I am good with money and make great financial decisions?

It's best to stick to one or two questions and write out your questions six times each night before going to sleep. Afformations are so powerful. I have laid many ghosts to rest and come up with some of my best ideas using them, as well as changing old negative beliefs that were holding me back from living my fucking incredible life, and we all deserve to be living our best lives!

When You're Tempted to Lock Up Your Daughters: Developing Empathy

The stepmother does have a few issues when it comes to empathy. She is so fixated on her own situation and making sure her daughters are OK that she is a right arse to Cinderella. They could have tried to see what it was like from their stepsister's standpoint, but all the women are too wrapped up in their personal dramas to even think about it.

We have all done it. Been so caught up in our own pain that we can't see what others are going through. Ricky Gervais's brilliant Netflix series *After Life* shows this so well as the main character is so submerged in his own grief and pain, he fails to see everyone around him has their own pain too. If you haven't seen it, I totally recommend it, even if you are not a Gervais fan.

It is so easy to say, 'Walk a mile in their shoes, then you'd know,' but who wants to walk in someone else's sweaty old boots? Luckily there is a much easier way to see things from someone else's viewpoint, not only in seeing how they feel but also in seeing yourself from their perspective. Scary as that may seem, it is such a game-changer.

Exercise
Walk a Mile in Their Manolo Blahniks

This is a classic NLP technique, and I often use it with clients. Set out three chairs or three cushions on the floor. Sit in the first seat and describe the issue or problem from your perspective. Then sit in the second seat as either the other person involved or the problem and tell it from that person's perspective. The third seat is neutral and offers the outsider's view. You could make the outsider an alien who doesn't have the usual social barriers and sees the whole thing from as far outside as possible, or how the entire situation would look to a stranger.

That's it, such a simple technique to explain how to do yet very powerful. I have yet to have a client where this doesn't completely alter how they see things. If you have no chairs, sit in three different places on the floor, but it is important that you physically change places. The brain accepts this and works with it. Talking out loud is best too. Look over to an empty chair or sitting area as if they are there. You may feel daft for a minute or two, but it is so cathartic to be able to pour your heart out and rant and rave that most people soon forget about feeling awkward and let rip.

When you are the second party, it may take a minute or two to get going. Being in a different chair and looking back at where you were sitting is helpful, so if you need a couple of breaths to get into their space, that's OK.

Before tackling the bigger stuff, you might want to test this exercise on something small, even if it's the dog. Imagine feeling pissed off with your dog begging for food or something, then seeing it from the dog's perspective of how-else-do-I-get-food?   You-are-the-food-giver-and-it-smells-so-good! But it really works wonders on bigger stuff!

I used this classic NLP technique myself after a banger of an argument with my other half. I had been so sure of my case; I was right, goddamn it! Then I did this exercise, and it was a revelation. I started seeing his side of things and also how the whole shit fest looked to an outsider, making me realise what ridiculous nonsense the whole thing was and how I had acted pretty badly. I can't even remember what the argument was about, but I could now see how we both were feeling and coming from. It didn't mean I was completely wrong, just as the stepmother isn't completely wrong to want a better life for her daughters, but I saw how I had made him feel and why he had been defensive.

The stepmother could maybe have seen how being an arse to Cinderella wasn't the best way to go about things and seen how this looked to an outsider. I'm not saying she would have instantly changed her ways. As a coach, I am guessing there was some exploring to do in her deeper stuff and beliefs, but it would have been a start.

Overview and Action Plan

- Negative self-limiting beliefs tend to be given to you as a kid, and THEY ARE UNTRUE.
- You can unwittingly pass on those beliefs to others without realising.
- Humans are wired to focus on negatives, but you can change that wiring.
- Seeing things from someone else's perspective can change everything and help you develop empathy.

Afformations

Refer to your positive statements list (see page 71-72) and create two or three afformations tailored to you.

Journal Prompts

- What old beliefs might be stopping me from being more of myself?
- How can I allow and give myself full permission to let go of those things that I need to let go of?
- What roles am I choosing to play?

Chapter Five

Overcoming Self-sabotage and Finding Your Council of Support

The Stepsisters: Owning Your Issues

OFTEN CALLED THE UGLY STEPSISTERS, although I always thought that was a bit unkind as no one is ugly, they just act ugly sometimes. Sure, even as a kid, I could see from the story that they were none too clever at interacting with others nicely at any level, even each other, but was that enough to make them ugly? The stepsisters' story seems to be that they lose their dad somehow, leaving just the girls and mum. Mum goes and marries some other bloke, I assume, to have some security. The guy already has a daughter, and the sisters behave rather crappy towards Cinderella, teasing, bullying and taking her nice stuff. On top of this, not only do they go to the ball without her but give her some miserable jobs while they party on down.

At the ball, it seems their facial recall is as bad as the prince when they fail to recognise her now she's had a wash and put a posh frock on. Then, to top it off, when the prince turns up for his foot fetish shoe try-on, they hide Cinderella to try and get the hot guy themselves, even tussling with each other over it. To be fair, I have been to the sales in shoe departments and have witnessed shoe fights with women trying to squeeze their size 8's into a size 5 shoe because, well, bargain! But jeez, these girls have issues.

Sabotaging Your Own Arse

Yet we are all the stepsisters at some point, or at the very least have known people like them. I know I was like them for a long time because what they are really doing is self-sabotage. You know the stuff. Saying today is the day that you'll start that diet, yet there are doughnuts in the office because it's Janice's birthday, so let's make tomorrow the day to start. Creating arguments in relationships ensures a split when the other person drops the L bomb and scares you shitless. Or starting fights because that was the only way you got Daddy's attention as a kid was when he shouted at you. Or, what it looks like the stepsisters do, you try and control others to the point of bullying and throwing in a big wad of make-them-feel-shit-because-deep-down-I-feel-shit for good measure.

Ah, wonderful self-sabotage, those thoughts and actions that really only hurt you. Yet you do them anyway because hidden in your subconscious is the memory that those actions worked once, or not to do them might attract bears into your life, but they only cause you emotional pain in the end too. Your life will stay where it is as you repeat old patterns, never being able to move on.

The stepsisters self-sabotage by exerting control over Cinderella. Control is a classic sabotage technique, along with the other usual suspects, procrastination, walking away if anything goes even slightly tits up, putting yourself down all the time, dating idiots and more. For the sisters, it seems as though controlling someone else plus making that person feel crap are their self-sabotaging tools of choice. A need for control is often down to wanting to feel safe and strong. Being in control feels good, whereas opening up to someone is way too scary. Showing vulnerability to someone? Hell no! Yet sharing vulnerabilities creates intimacy and forms the strongest bonds in all types of relationships. Dogs rolling over for a belly rub is a bonding thing. There is no more vulnerable behaviour for a dog than to offer up its softest, most physically vulnerable parts for a damn good rubbing. If a dog can roll over and display its belly and balls when it wants to say hi to you on a deeper level, then you can do it too (metaphorically speaking or getting around the supermarket will take ages) no matter how uncomfortable. If the sisters have lost their dad and had no choice about having a new one or indeed another sister, it is not really surprising that controlling parts of their life would help them feel better. But as shit, as it was for Cinderella, it does the sisters no good for themselves either.

Control was just one of my own self sabotaging actions. When I used to work with kids at a primary school, they used to call me Miss Do-it-herself because I always wanted to take over and do it myself. I found it so hard to just leave them to it, draw their own posters, make their own models, anything. These were seven-year-old kids, for god's sake, yet I still wanted to take over and do it because I could do it better. How awful a confession is that!

It didn't stop with the kids I worked with either. My daughter suffered, too – although I was oblivious at the time. I thought I was doing a good job at creating an independent child, leaving her to put together flatpack furniture (a bedside cabinet she wanted, not furniture for the whole house, that would have been a bit over the top), or smiling at her attempts to cook dinner and letting her decorate the Christmas tree.

Yet, I now realise that these moments were when I *chose* them, not every day. I was controlling the moments of 'lack' of control. I was a monster! She knew I rearranged the tree decorations after she had gone to bed. I still have the odd moment today, such as being overly fussy about Christmas tree ornament placement or checking the front door is locked before I go to bed despite my husband saying he has done it. Now, if the odd old habit pops out like that, I spot it and name it out loud, apologising to the person involved and being okay in being vulnerable by saying how much I appreciate their help in stopping this side of me. And those little issues do pop out now and again, like an old man's testicles from a pair of Speedos, just when you think you have everything covered and safely sorted, occasionally one may slip past your safety gusset and be on view. Still, if those around you know you have this happen now and again, they will soon quietly tell you and let you quietly tuck it away whilst they politely looking the other way. This is why it is so helpful to share your vulnerability with those in your circle. They can help you get that slip-out back where it belongs, with love and subtlety, and let you work on what caused the slippage.

Repeating Old Patterns

Why do we do these things to ourselves? Who in their right mind would sabotage their own happiness? Well, it's that 'in their right mind' bit that is the problem. Your subconscious remembers behaviours that worked for you in the past, behaviours that helped you gain something, that made you feel good or, at the very least, stopped you feeling bad. Your brain then created patterns to use in similar situations, or old emotions were provoked. The trouble really starts when your circumstances change, but the behaviour patterns remain. You repeat those same old patterns because they worked for you way back then.

When I was an artist, I shared studio space with around half a dozen other artists. It was a gorgeous place, an old print works in the castle grounds in Reigate, Surrey. We would hold a public exhibition once a year and always got a great turnout. In my first year, I set up my display and was dead chuffed with how it looked. I could almost pass as a real artist! (I had yet to work on my negative self-beliefs back then.) Slowly the public began to arrive for the opening night, which was always the busiest as there was free wine and Surrey people swoop on that sort of shit like flies to an old toffee. A group of people had gathered at my artwork and were discussing it, the free booze aiding happy talk and complimentary remarks. (Yes, yes, I know, it was also because my work was damned good.) So, what did my brain have me do? Stand on a plinth and soak up those compliments? Stand in front of the crowd and describe how it all came about and my inner workings? Or did I stand at the back of the crowd, pretending to be a member of the public, making mumbling comments along with them before waddling off to look at other people's work? Standing in front of my work and declaring myself the artist may have incited critique, which of course, I would take as a critique of *me*, not my work. And what if they laughed at the very idea of me presenting myself as an artist? Oh, imposter syndrome, you huge self-saboteur you! So, yes, I hid. I stayed quiet and hoped that no one would notice me as I mumbled 'rhubarb' amidst the group, nodded sagely and wandered off.

This behaviour had worked for me as a small kid, and my subconscious remembered. I remembered that staying quiet and not attracting attention saved me from my mum's wrath, saved me ridicule at school and saved me the pain of rejection. My brain had learned that it saved me from no end of terrible, life-threatening bear situations, such as Vicky laughing at me in the girls changing room because I had a training bra with blue hippos on. I bloody loved that bra, but I was the first to get one when I woke up one morning with a fair pair of boobs without any warning when I was 10 years old. They were a shock. My mum had teeny tits, and I have a strong childhood memory of her pushing her palms together as she sang, 'I must, I must, I must improve my bust. I will, I will, I'll make them bigger still. Surprise, surprise, they grow before your eyes.' So, her daughter suddenly having a rack must have seemed completely unfair to her, and little comments were often thrown into the daily chatter, creating a sense of shame in my new shape. Adding laughter from my peers, along with a boy pulling my top down in the school field, made me an expert at making myself invisible and unnoticed to avoid such scrutiny.

All these memories didn't come flooding back to me on a conscious level as I stood in that crowd at my exhibition. Still, the old subconscious was doing what it does best, scanning past experiences, seeing what worked before and creating a similar behaviour that helped back then. Amazingly I did sell a couple of pictures, and there are few joys better than seeing red dots on your work. Still, I wonder how many more I could have sold or how many collectors I could have gained if I had stood at the front there and claimed myself the artist, having witty banter with everyone and being the Belle of the Ball.

Okay, I may have stretched the what-ifs there, but you never know! And there's the rub. You will never know what could be if you keep playing the same old record, the same old behaviour. Because in repeating old patterns, you are keeping yourself stuck, sabotaging all your glittery, awesome possibilities. The good news? It is possible to disrupt and stop self-sabotaging behaviour and thought patterns with a little effort. I had to add that caveat 'with a little effort' because it can be uncomfortable looking deep enough inside yourself to spot the little buggers, those patterns of behaviour that you would much rather not poke about near because they are sore. The pain is why we prefer to avoid the issue altogether until something bad happens, and we have to go to the clinic to get our sore areas looked at.

Trigger (Not) Happy

When you sit down and really think about the areas of your life where you fuck up or are most unhappy or grumpy, you slowly begin to spot some common factors. I spotted that keeping quiet made me feel pretty bad deep in my gut. I felt irritated with myself for not speaking up or with others because I felt unheard. Inside I was screaming all the things I wanted to say but never managed to vocalise. As well as feeling crappy when I kept quiet, I felt bad after giving up too soon on things too, such as new business ideas or handing my notice in at jobs where I felt bored and unfulfilled, and afterwards still feeling bored and unfulfilled. (And just now, I was feeling it whilst eating Ramen noodles.) Those reactionary actions didn't help me in any way, they just kept me stuck, and I had no one to blame but myself. When I poked a bit deeper, looking for my triggers, that is when I consciously remembered all those times how staying quietly invisible helped me when I was a kid. All those times, my subconscious remembered but not thought to mention them to my conscious brain as it thought it had everything in hand by repeating those behaviours to keep us safe from possible bear attacks. So to repeat:

The 'with a little effort' part is the slightly uncomfortable feeling of looking inside yourself and starting to recognise your behaviours and triggers.

Keeping a journal helped with this. Every time I uncovered a trigger, I wrote it down and looked at it hard to understand its source. Then I would try and come up with a couple more positive reactions that I could use to kick those old sabotaging ones in the knackers until they decided to just not bother turning up. I learned to spot the churning in my belly as the signal that a button had been pushed and would take a breath and tell myself that it was an old button, that it was no longer my circus, and they were definitely no longer my monkeys. I would take a minute to try and see what it was about the situation that wasn't working for me and what I needed to do to be awesome.

A great trick to help blast them away was to write the negative statement in my journal and then, in red ink, write a response as if it were a court of law reply. Did the statement stand up in court? Was the evidence false or inadmissible? For me, there were no statements that were accepted by 'the court'. Either it was hearsay with no proof, or the source had no credibility; it was amazing. I would write something like 'Nobody wants to hear what I have to say, why would they?' then flip my head over to court mode and in red ink write: 'The court sees no evidence to support this statement. No witnesses can be called up to support this. The court, therefore, dismisses this statement as inadmissible and requests it be struck from the records.' Somehow, looking at my negative belief in the cold light of a courtroom and needing to provide supporting evidence made me see the belief as to the falsehood it was. Actually, writing down a formal dismissal gave me permission to dismiss it.

Finding Your Inner Council: What Would Dolly Say?

I have two photos pinned up in my workspace. Most people would guess they are of my husband and daughter or maybe Jesus and Buddha or some other spiritual figurehead, but they are Dolly Parton and RuPaul, and I don't apologise for that! These are two people who I hold in high regard, right up there with all the top gurus or spiritual leaders. I see Dolly as a lovely, warm human being who is so loving and giving, one of the best songwriters and a hard-arsed businesswoman who knows what she wants and doesn't take any shit from anyone. RuPaul is a model, singer, actor, TV personality and the queen of all drag queens. He tells it straight and expects people to be their most fabulous yet is kind in his gentle pushing to get those who don't believe in themselves to realise how fabulous they are. What is there not to adore about either of these people? With their photos in front of me, I can look at them and visualise what they would say to me in any situation; they are my little council of fabulousness. Dolly tells me to go for my goals without wavering but treat those involved around me with love. RuPaul tells me, 'Good-luck-and-don't-fuck-it-up," meaning go for it with all you have, don't doubt yourself and your inner awesome.

When it comes to self-sabotage, having an inner council, people that will never judge you negatively, is a real bonus. These people will point out self-limiting thoughts or behaviour or make you feel better if you feel low in the old self-esteem or confidence area. They are a voice you trust and hold in high regard, so I would take in their supportive comments. Picture them right in front of you, cheering you on or telling you, 'You've got this.' Or that's what mine says, and it really does flip my emotions or thoughts. Who would be your council? I'd love to know

---

Exercise
Get Your Needs Met

Self-sabotaging behaviour usually means some emotional need is not being met. For the stepsisters, it looks as though fear of loss and a lack of control creates their own controlling behaviour. Working out what needs are not being met in your life is an important step in beating the arse of self-sabotage. Journal the fuck out of possible reasons and identifying those needs that are not being acknowledged or given what they need. Whenever something or someone pushes your buttons, look deep into the possible reasons and what is not being met for you. Below is a list of possibilities, but it is by no means exhaustive.

- acceptance
- appreciation
- awareness
- challenge
- communion
- contribution
- closeness
- compassion
- creativity
- efficacy
- equality
- growth
- honesty
- independence
- intimacy
- love
- movement/exercise
- participation
- presence
- safety
- space

- affection
- authenticity
- beauty
- choice
- competence
- cooperation
- community
- consideration
- discovery
- effectiveness
- food
- harmony
- humour
- inspiration
- joy
- meaning
- nurturing
- peace
- purpose
- security
- spontaneity

- air
- autonomy
- belonging
- clarity
- consciousness
- communication
- companionship
- consistency
- ease
- empathy
- freedom
- hope
- inclusion
- integrity
- learning
- mourning
- order
- play
- respect
- self-expression
- stability

- stimulation
- to be known
- to see and be seen
- to be understood
- water
- sexual expression
- shelter
- understanding

- support to know
- to matter
- to understand
- trust
- warmth - rest/sleep
- safety
- touch

Get in the habit of writing down and exploring the whats and whys of anything that pisses you off or irritates you.
- What is it about it that is really bugging you?
- Why do you think that is?
- What need is not being met?

Then, importantly:
- What can you do to address this?
- Can you change anything, put something in place or do you just need to breathe and let it go, knowing it is not in your circle of control and that's okay; you don't need to control everything?

Learning to live with uncertainty is a wonderful release. Sure, it's scary sometimes, but it's OK. It's all OK.

Overview and Action Plan

- Self-sabotage stops you from having the awesome life you should be living.
- Be gentle with yourself as you start to look at your triggers.
- What needs are not being met? Remember your core values (see Chapter 3, page 00) because it is possibly one of those.
- Start journaling triggers as they come up.
- Be open to being vulnerable but again, go easy on yourself.
- You've got this, you are fabulous, and I believe in you.
- A mental council of positive support helps shift any dips and will cheer you on to be fucking fabulous.
- It's OK. It's all OK.

Afformations

- Why do I find it so easy to remember my core values and not put blocks in their way?
- Why do I find it easy to forgive my past and those in it and move forward feeling happier and more peaceful? (Yeah, this one again, but it is sooooo good!)

Journal Prompts

- What does my soul need?
- What is it that is bugging me about this situation/person/behaviour?
- What needs do I have that are not being met here?

Chapter Six

Conjuring Up Your Own Inner Magic, Called Confidence

The Fairy Godmother: Saving Yourself

WHERE DID THE IDEA OF A FAIRY GODMOTHER come from? That idea of someone whose sole purpose in life is to grant your wishes, with no life of their own, we assume. I mean, are they away doing their own thing only to be whisked away at any given moment to sort out your shit when you yell? I love the fairy godmother in *Shrek* – she has an actual thriving business, awesome. But on the whole, these magical women (and they mostly are female, if you are male and in that line of business you probably live in a lamp and demand to be rubbed before doing any wish-granting malarkey) seem to exist solely for us, which is a nice thought but rather unfair on them.

But if they are there just for us, why the hell do they seem to only turn up at stupid times? Why on earth didn't she turn up for Cinderella as soon as she was born, like they did for Sleeping Beauty. Even if Sleeping Beauty's lot did give her rather impractical stuff like being beautiful, although the good singing voice could have been useful. Maybe the third fairy was about to give her the gift of good business sense and a kick-arse recording contract before huffy pants Maleficent stormed in with her knickers in a twist for not getting an invite.

The idea of fairies and spirits is as old as the hills, both the ones that help us and those determined to make life a pain in the arse. It seems that the idea of fairy godmothers has a bit of a religious root (I guess the 'god' part of the word gives that away), and they really started to appear in the Middle Ages when the role of godparents was pretty important. In stories earlier than Charles Perrault's 1697 telling of *Cinderella* and *Sleeping Beauty,* there are no fairies. Grimm's *Cinderella* has the ghost of her dead mum helping her and, even weirder, the Chinese version, *Ye Xian,* has the ghost of a pet fish sent by her dead mum.

No dead fish for our Cinderella, the fairy godmother turns up when she wants to go to a party but can't. I will give this fairy godmother the benefit of the doubt and suggest that maybe she was waiting for Cinderella to show a bit of backbone and get her arse in gear. But got so fed-up waiting, she just gave her the goddam dress and taxi to the party, hoping she could then bugger off and go give that genie a rub.

Job Role: Your Own Fairy Godmother

So, is it frustrating being a fairy godmother? To be given that role and watch as your charge turns into a big drip? If someone has trusted you enough to ask you to be a responsible adult in a child's life, do you just wait until they are falling apart before stepping in? I'm going to repeat the idea that the existence of a fairy godmother is one big mindfuck, and maybe we have been our own fairy godmother all along. What if that has been a part of our inner selves all along, the part that comes up with solutions to our life questions? Then wouldn't we be crazy not to use her sooner rather than wait until the world is falling around our heads? If we don't know of her existence, it is fair enough not to call on her. When it comes to things like this, we are not taught it by parents or teachers. Parents tend to worry more about teaching you to say please and thank you, how to use the toilet (which is something to always be thankful to them for) and how to cross a road without dying, another pretty good one. Sure, sometimes they throw in the odd curve ball such as how to hide from the rent man, that you should never talk to strangers. (I was taught that one, and it took me until my own child at three years old told me off for talking to the cashier at the supermarket to realise the message should be never *go off* with strangers.) Talking to strangers is a perfectly normal, sociable human interaction. I then changed tack to teaching my daughter to trust her gut instinct. If she felt uncomfortable about someone, trust that feeling, even if you can't put your finger on why. After all, teachers have enough on their plate teaching us to read, write and add up without having time to worry about our psychological make-up. (Although some schools are starting to teach mindfulness and focus on self-esteem, which I adore.) So, we tend to find this stuff out for ourselves, often from self-help books, Google and YouTube, the tools for nearly all adulting needs.

If we are lucky, we spot issues and seek help from a therapist or coach, a kind of paid-for fairy godmother who uses their skills and training in helping us understand and deal with shit. No magic wand for them, just years of training and a ton of experience in this stuff. Some of us stumble across wise authors such as Susan Jeffers Steven. R. Covey, Tony Robbins and others who have written down their knowledge so they can get it to as many people as possible. If this is you, I do need to remind you about the fairy godmother mindfuck again here. You know? The one where there is no magic wand? There are some amazing, life-altering books out there, but just having them on your bookshelf having skimmed through doesn't work. You need to read them thoroughly, a few times if possible, but then DO what they suggest! I repeat:

There is no magic wand; it is up to you to put the work in. In fact, it is only after you put the work in that you get to see a bit of magic, the magic of your life being so fucking awesome you could burst.

That is where the real magic is, in creating a life so wonderful that it is a joy to get up in the morning. A life so full of contentment that you glow. Think this is impossible? Not on your sweet Nelly! I dare you put everything in place to get to where you want to be in life and come back to me saying, 'Meh!'

Is All This Magic, Everything It's Cracked Up to Be?

What about those of us who try to be that fairy godmother? When my ex-husband and I split up, our daughter was only seven years old. I had such guilt for not being able to give her the perfect family life. You know, mum always there cooking and sewing, dad working away in the barn, us kids running across the fields under a vast blue, cloudless sky, laughing and playing. Each night we fell into our beds, happy and exhausted, calling goodnight to each other... Wait, that's the fucking *Little House on the Prairie* and *The Waltons!* I got my view of a perfect family from TV! So, in reality, I had no idea what a perfect family looked like. Still, I was so desperate to give her a lovely life that rather than budget and make sure we were OK, I rented a stupidly big house in a lovely commuter suburb so I could pretend everything was fine and fabulous. There was no way I could keep that house for long, but I wanted to wave a wand and grant my daughter what I thought was a lovely life.

Overcompensating is a common thing to do, but it never actually does the person on the receiving end any good in the long run. We would all love to just magic away our loved ones hurt and pain with a swoosh of a wand and make their whole world covered in glitter. But life just ain't like that, not real, everyday life. There is no such thing as a perfect family, a perfect parent/lover/sister/friend, whatever. The world is full of a wild mix of nice, bad, painful, joyful, disappointing, exhilarating stuff, and is what being alive is all about. We need to accept we will all fuck up on occasion, sometimes royally so. Everyone does, even heads of state, archbishops, film stars, everyone. Tabloids and gossip magazines make a fortune from it and even totally make some up, such as what size we *should* be or what clothes people *should* have worn. Can you imagine one of the gossip magazines doing a spread on Cinderella? Telling us how she beat the odds in a riches to rags to riches again story, asking who made the dress, vilifying the stepmother and sisters, *Hello* magazine getting an exclusive on the wedding?

Anyway, we think if we magic away all the bad stuff for our loved ones, then they will be happy, but it just makes things worse as when bad things happen to them as they go through life, they have no idea how to cope and what to do. Anything from someone dying to not getting a job they wanted. Negatives on any scale will be a shock to them. We need to learn how to cope with everything life throws at us and do stuff for ourselves. So not only is the idea of waiting for a fairy godmother to haul your arse away from whatever mess you've found yourself in a pointless one but trying to be that fairy godmother for someone is not the way to go either. To be a fully rounded, emotionally okay human being, you need to experience everything, even the crappier bits and learn from that experience. The best thing you can do for other people is not to shield them from life but to simply be there, a rock in a storm or to share the sunshine and laughter.

My nan died from a heart attack when I was 14, and she was a mere 57. We were close, she lived in the same town as me, and I saw her often. The way I received the news was from another, a fairly distant relative who stopped me as I walked to school, told me nan was gone and went on her merry way. Not sure what to do, I carried on to school. During a geography lesson a little later, it hit me, and I broke down. The teacher looked terrified as a friend explained the issue, and he sent me to the office so he could carry on with his oxbow lakes and the population of New Brazil. He never approached me again to find out how I was. In the office, I was given a chair over in the corner, out of everyone's way, and I assume someone was called. I may have just been sent home by myself. I don't remember much else apart from a tearful mum turning up briefly (she didn't live with us), and then no one really spoke about it again. We were not taken to the funeral as it was thought to be too sad for us. It took me years to come to terms with the fact she was really was dead. It took me three more decades to be OK with showing tears and grief. From how everyone had acted, my teachers and family members, I took in that people didn't like to see you sad and grieving; it was something to hide. If I had been able to go to the funeral, I would have understood she was gone, grieved and laughed at the glorious memories of her along with everyone else. It is the purpose of funerals and wakes.

I would have learned it was okay to be sad and show it. Shit happens, people die, such is the circle of life. Not my lot, they tried to protect me from all that, but in trying to magic away all that sad stuff, all I learned was to hide sadness and tears as something bad. These days I can happily snivel away at the drop of a hat, even an advert for cat food. I am at peace with my tears, and they flow at most things, happy, sad, just plain old emotional. When I watched the film *Big Fish,* my daughter came running downstairs thinking some awful news had come, such was my wailing. So be a big old rock, not a fairy godmother.

It is so much more useful to stop waiting for that fairy godmother to turn up. She was right there in the mirror all along.

Becoming Your Own Fairy Godmother

So how do you go about discovering and becoming your very own fairy godmother? Combining the first three characters, Cinderella, the stepmother and the stepsisters, is a start. With Cinderella, we looked at creating actual goals instead of dreaming, stepping out of your comfort zone and discovering your true core values. With the stepmother, we tackled negative self-beliefs, and with the stepsisters, we looked at self-sabotage. In doing all those things, you are well on your way to becoming an invincible badass. But what if we could magic up some confidence too? Cinderella must have felt shit-hot in that dress with an instant confidence boost. Imagine being able to do it that quickly? There is a way I may not be conjuring up a Vera Wang for you to party on down in, but there is a way of learning to flip on a confidence switch simply by stepping into it. Imagine if you could create a power circle right in front of you that you simply stepped into, and boom! Confident you.

Exercise
The Power Circle of Confidence

This technique takes a bit of practice, but once you've got it, you can start creating your own kick-arse magic.

1. Think of a time when you felt damned good and confident. It doesn't matter how far back you need to go.; you just need to remember the situation and how you felt.

2. Now, stand up, close your eyes and visualise a circle on the floor right in front of you. Make it a good size that

will be easy to stand in the middle of, maybe about 3ft in diameter.

3. Now, make that circle your favourite colour and make it bright and glorious.

4. As you stand there, go back in your mind and remember a time when you felt confident and fabulous. For me, I went back to a party in my teens when I felt hot to trot, but it can be any time for you. That time you rocked the meeting, when you were flying going down a hill on your bike, when you told that joke that had the whole room in stitches. In fact, anytime you felt buzzed with that feeling of really owning it and feeling great.

5. As you remember feeling confident, really focus on what you saw, what you felt, what you heard, smelled, everything. Now ramp all those sensations, the sounds, brightness, faces, colours, and really relive that moment, how amazing you felt.

6. Notice how good it all feels and as the feeling intensifies, step into that bright circle in front of you. Take in how you are feeling, what you can see and hear, any sounds and smells, your posture, your breathing, everything.

7. When the good feeling is at its height, step out of the circle, leaving all those feelings and emotions still in the circle. Open your eyes and really come out of the visualisation (this is called breaking state, which just means coming back to the now). Repeat the steps a few times, breaking state each time you step out again.

Your subconscious will remember the feeling of stepping into that circle and bring it back instantly whenever you picture that circle and step into it. I like to picture it outside the door to rooms I am about to enter for meetings or talks. I step into the circle, breathe for a couple of seconds while all that buzz comes back and then carry it through into the room. You can repeat the exercise as often as you like or need, plus the circle is limitless, so you can add as much fuck-off awesome confidence as you like each time. I also get clients to look ahead to events or situations they know they have coming up where they want to feel confident.

By visualising the future event, I get them to see what they would like to see, hear what they would like to hear, any smells or tastes and to see it all just before the moment they need that confidence boost so that they will know the moment to step into their circle. One client wanted it to avoid falling apart in her divorce proceedings, and she aced it, looking cool and confident while her ex spluttered and got in a twist. A friend of mine used it for a wedding speech he was dreading, remembering when he was telling a silly story to mates in the school playground and how they had listed and laughed. Repeating stepping in and out of the circle will check your results and add to the strength of the magic. There, you can now magic up your own amazing instant confidence. Who needs a fairy godmother?

Overview and Action Plan

- Your fairy godmother was deep inside you all along; stop waiting for her to show up and save you.
- Trying to be some else's fairy godmother might do more harm than good; show them they are their own fairy godmother.
- Learn to use the instant confidence boost spell!

Afformations

- How am I stronger than I ever thought possible?
- Why do I radiate confidence and self-belief?
- What do I need to do to realise my potential?

Journal Prompts

- What do I need to give myself permission to believe I have the power to grant my own dreams?
- What am I still blocking?
- What would a day in the life of super confident me look like?

Chapter Seven

Navigating Obsession and Turning It to Your Advantage

The Prince:
Learning to Let Go

THE PRINCE DOESN'T HAVE THE LEAD ROLE in fairy stories and rarely makes the headline title. Yet he always seems needed for a happy ever after ending. It is always down to the prince to save the day, whether by fighting off dragons, slashing his way through enchanted forests or simply giving some unsuspecting woman a snog, often without even asking first, never mind a couple of glasses of Merlot and a fancy-coming-back-to-mine. Sometimes, even if the poor woman appears dead and in some odd glass coffin in the woods. If she looks helpless or the tiniest bit princess-like, he'll snog her. It isn't just guys with this problem; some lady dudes go around kissing pond life. Although, to be fair, we have all been there after a few too many glasses of fizz. Fairy-tale land sure is fucked up sometimes.

As a prince, he is not in complete control of his lot. He doesn't have his own kingdom yet and lives in the shadow of his dad, with marriage seemingly the route to becoming his own man. The prince's story in *Cinderella* is that he goes along with his parents' decision that it's time to get married. Oh, and by the way, you must make your choice of a lifelong Mrs this weekend at a party where we have sent an invite to every well-to-do girl in town telling them you want to snog and marry one of them, OK? And you thought your parents were embarrassing!

The prince goes along with it because this is how things are done. His parents/social rules are that he joins up with a hot chick because maybe a singleton prince couldn't run a piss up in a brewery, let alone a kingdom and producing sprogs is a big thing for royalty. Now, when he does clock Cinderella and gets a gun in his pocket, rather than accept that she chose to leave without swapping numbers, as is her prerogative, he chases her and finds her shoe. Instead of letting it all go and heading back to the ballroom full of readily available women, he becomes obsessed with the idea of this one unknown, unavailable woman, and he goes to ridiculous efforts to get her.

The Hat Shall Be Mine!

How many of us have latched on to an idea so hard that we forget about everything else? As a young teen, about 13 years, I loved a TV show called *Citizen Smith* starring Robert Lyndsey as an unemployed dreamer called 'Wolfie' Smith living in Tooting, London. Wolfie's hero is Che Guevara and the idea of being a revolutionist, even wearing a similar beret to the one Che wears. I decided that I couldn't leave the house until I had a beret with a star stud, like Wolfie and Che. I fixated on that beret. Life got put on hold. I refused to socialise until I had that beret. How could I? That beret would change my life, so of course, I couldn't be seen until I possessed it.

Eventually, I bought an old beret from an army surplus and put a metal star stud on the front. To this day, I remember how I felt putting that beret on, how tall I walked, how I was sure everyone now regarded me with awe and wonder.

'Our own Che Guevara, here in deepest Surrey!' they would surely gasp. That weekend I graced the local youth disco with my presence after many weeks away. I strode in with my glorious, felted crown upon my head, fully expecting the crowds to part and the whispers to start. Nothing happened, not even a glance. No one gave a flying fuck about the object of my desire, that thing that I had obsessed over, lusted after (as much as a 13-year-old can lust after anything, which is actually pretty fucking intensely, you should have seen my love for David Essex or Les from The Bay City Rollers).

I had missed weeks of the youth club and discos due to my deluded focus on this beret. Weeks where I could have had laughs, loves, learned the latest group dance and generally had a bloody good time. Instead, I had hidden away and sulked until I got that stupid hat. Actually, it was a pretty cool hat, it would be fun if I still had it, to be honest, but that is all, fun. It was definitely not worth hiding away from life for. I can still recall the intensity of my longing for it, how I thought life would be awesome once I had it. I remember the feeling of confidence I had wearing it, too. How I walked a bit taller and looked people straight in the eye with a knowing smile. But what did I miss while I was so blinded by the obsession of owning it?

Obsession: Loved-up at First Sight

Those good feelings I remember are probably what the prince felt when he first set eyes on Cinderella, and they danced. We all remember our first crushes and how strongly we felt. My first crushes were The Virginian and Captain Scarlet. I was too young to understand what a crush was. I just knew that my tummy tickled, and nothing else existed in my world when they were on. I *luuuurved* them!

I was six when I asked Father Christmas for a cowboy outfit, so I could be The Virginian, and again, I remember how wonderful I felt when wearing it: hat tilted so far forwards over my eyes that I had to crane my neck back to see anything. As an adult, I always fancied dark-haired men, my husband is dark-haired, so I guess I never did forget my first crushes. We have all obsessed over something in our lives, unable to think of anything else, brain turning something over and over. Maybe it was something someone said, and you can't stop thinking about what they meant or what you could have said back. Maybe it was an ex, which you stalked on social media for weeks after they dumped you, visiting places you know they go to on the off chance you bump into them again in the hope they realise what an idiot they were; you were the one all along. Of course, it will never happen, a part of you knows that, but the thing is that obsession is like an addiction – at first, it is so fabulous that all you focus on is how good it feels. You then start neglecting other parts of your life, such as not seeing friends or going out to focus solely on this wonderful thing. You start to drop things that you enjoyed before but, in the raptures of your newfound obsession, seem to be less enjoyable. The new thing starts to become all-consuming. If that object of the obsession is taken away, then we are completely lost; life holds nothing else for us because we have stopped doing other things. This is where people start to ruminate, have dark, unhelpful thoughts going round and round in their heads.

Believing only one thing will make you happy is a delusional idea, and if that goes too, you are lost

---

Exercise
Recognising Obsession

If you think you might currently be running an obsession, this exercise can help you understand its consequences.

1. Take a piece of paper and divide it into nine squares.

2. Write down something in every square that makes up your life, such as family, friends, hobbies, things that bring you joy etc. Remove any one of them, and you still have lots of things in your life.

3. Put the object of your obsession in a box and have the others blank because you have slowly dumped all the other things that filled those boxes. The friends have been dropped, the family, things that usually gave you pleasure before are empty as you stopped doing them, so all you have is a lone square with your obsession in it.

4. See how that on its own makes for a rather unfulfilling life, but what if that disappeared too? Your life would feel completely empty, and you would feel devastated that the only thing you relied on for happiness was now gone.

The key is to keep that sheet of paper filled with different things. With your life full, it is healthy to take breaks now and again from your mission and go to one of the things listed. Use the following exercise (see page 118) to help you develop new activities and hobbies to keep those boxes full.

A Little Bit of Obsession Can Be Healthy

The prince, unlike Cinderella, has a goal, but his sense of loss and feeling powerless, along with his sudden happiness being whipped away from him pretty darned quick and not understanding why clouds his judgement a bit. His goal and way of achieving it were not particularly healthy, and it doesn't look like anyone around him would tell him. This may sound a bit gloomy, but what if I told you how you could turn things around and make obsession something pretty damned awesome that could help you achieve your positive, fabulous goals? Not any goals of getting that arsehole who dumped you back, or anything like that, but goals that will elevate you to fabulousness?

You see, to achieve something, you need to be just a little bit obsessed with an outcome. Wanting something badly enough can give you motivation and drive, the creativity and ingenuity to solve any difficulty. When I look back to how much I wanted that Che Guevara/Citizen Smith beret and stop looking at how daft I was at hiding from life until I got it, I realise that I had actually worked out how to get one due to my obsession with it.

Now, this was the 1970's, there was no Amazon or Google,

I had to work out how to make it happen. I realised the type of beret I wanted wasn't a fashion item but a military type. I then remembered an army surplus shop at the end of Surrey Street market in Croydon, just a half-hour bus ride from home. For a couple of weeks, instead of heading straight off to the record shop after my Saturday job at the local greengrocers and spending my entire pay packet on two albums, I saved my money. (I earned £6 a day, and way back then, when records were made of dinosaur bones, albums were £3, perfect!). Then off I trundled, battling my way through the crowded Surrey Street market in search of my goal, much like a prince hacking his way through a forest in search of a damsel in distress. Shouts of 'b'na-a-a-anas, pound a pound!' and 'Knickers! Get yer knickers here ladies!' from street traders could not distract me in my quest for the holy grail of a beret, even if those knickers were indeed a great deal. I pushed through the gangs of nanas with their wheeled shopping trollies, normally as scary as any gang of youths, but not today, today I was on a mission.

I made it to the army surplus store and stepped inside. I can still conjure up that distinct musty smell of decades-old dust, with a hint of prepubescence and middle-aged bloke that was their customer base. I only knew the shop existed because my younger brother and his mates were into old German army shirts back then. I was the only girl in there but was undaunted. I scanned this strange new territory and spotted the counter, hidden amongst strange paraphernalia I didn't recognise nor understand, but they were not my end goal, so my brain dismissed them quickly. Trying to sound knowledgeable and confident, I muttered 'Berets?' at the guy behind the counter. Without even looking up, he pointed to the end of the counter. And there they were! Plonked in a haphazard pile as if they were just more old crap rather than my heart's desire. Not quite the golden fleece moment I had imagined, but my sense of achievement was the same. Goal achieved; prize found. As I went to pay, I muttered about finding a star for the front, like Che's. The guy reaches under the desk and throws down a small cardboard box full of star studs. He is still engrossed in whatever he is reading and can't see my utter amazement at this small treasure chest of silver. This thing I had considered a distant dream, this object of my obsession, was nothing to him. I took one, paid and left feeling totally intoxicated.

At home, I put the star on the beret and stared at my reflection in the mirror. I had fucking done it! I had the same beret as Che and Wolfie. From this moment on, life would never be the same. But of course, life was exactly the same, just with a warmer head, although I didn't work that one out until later at the youth club.

My obsession with that hat had given me the inspiration to find one. OK, as goals go, that was a small one, but hey, I was 13! I worked out exactly what I wanted and ways I could make it happen. My adoration and need to possess that hat gave me the kick up the arse I needed to make it happen. The Afghan coat Wolfie wore didn't have that effect. I couldn't give two hoots about having one of those (my uncle gave me one a few years later, one he used to wear in the 1960s, it stank). Nope, I had a single goal that I turned into a mission and achieved it.

This is where you can make an obsession work for you. If that end game is a healthy goal, one that you have checked to make sure it doesn't affect anyone else negatively, that it is a healthy mission rather than an obsession. You may or may not want to check it with others first. They don't need to share your passion for the outcome, but if they raise certain concerns or arrange an intervention, take a second look at things, but remember that in the end, their approval is not strictly needed as this is your goal not theirs. Check that the goal has a positive outcome for you, then the *need* to achieve that goal can get you the determination and drive to go get it. It can help you think creatively about what is needed and the ingenuity to work out how to put that into place. If the want is strong enough, it helps you focus on the goal and helps you remember *why* you want it, and the why's are an important part of keeping motivated.

The main challenge is making any obsession a positive rather than a negative so that you control it rather than it controlling you.

Exercise
Keeping Healthy Control

Distracting yourself from the obsession now and again not only helps with not becoming overly immersed in that one thing but helps remind you of the other things in your life that are important too. Read a book, call someone, go to a cafe and people watch whilst having a mocha and a muffin, watch a film at the cinema, visit family, start a little hobby – anything! Use the following exercise to help you discover fresh activities.

1. Create a list of activities you enjoy, for example going to a café, baking, rummaging in second-hand stores or reading a book. Have at least 20 things on the list.

2. Now create a list of ways to interact with others. This could be anything from calling or messaging to a games night or cinema visit. Any way you enjoy contact with others.

3. Make sure you do one of the things from each list at least once a day. It need only be for 10 minutes, although longer is fine. Once the new activity becomes part of your daily routine, it becomes something you enjoy that is an addition to your obsession/goal, and keep in contact with people, even with a simple text to say 'Hi!' to a friend.

Take a Break to Stay on Track

Keeping those boxes in your life full will make it all the sweeter when you achieve your end game. Moreover, having your obsession/goal broken down into steps makes it easier to stay on track. Every time one of those steps is accomplished, take a break and celebrate somehow. This is a way of telling your brain that you are moving towards your goal. Go do something else that would benefit from your attention before getting down to the next step. Learning how to ground yourself is a healthy thing to add to your life and especially so when you are highly focused on a goal or mission.

Whilst writing this book, I made it part of the process to step away every 90 minutes to breathe and get some feeling in my arse again as I had been sat on it, lost in pouring out my brain onto the page. I have a playlist on Spotify I found called 'The Ultimate Happy Playlist', and I would put it on loud and make myself dance like a loon around the room until my energy changed.

As the days went by, my brain and body recognised what was occurring through repetition, and my energy would change as soon as I started my first bop about the room. Meditate (I use guided ones on YouTube), learn some breathing techniques, walk around the block, anything that is physically different or is in fresh surroundings will give your brain something else to focus on for a while and bring you back from becoming too sucked into that obsession or mission yet keep you fresh to go at it in an awesome, kick-arse way.

Get just a little obsessed with creating your best life and realising just how kick-arse awesome you are.

Overview and Action Plan

- Obsession can be put to good use if you control it and can become a healthy, positive activity rather than an unhealthy and controlling one.
- Make sure your goal doesn't affect anyone negatively. Check it is healthy and positive, that you can afford it etc. Never stop the rest of your life in pursuit of it.
- Take a breather now and again and do something different.

Afformations

- How do I easily recognise how positive my goals are and love how simply I can let go of any negatives?
- What do I need to do to have a full and happy life?
- Why do I enjoy the journey to achieving my goal as much as reaching my goal?

Journal Prompts

- What do I believe about this goal?
- What am I ignoring when it comes to this?
- What are the reasons for me to love this goal?

Chapter Eight

Finding Your Masculine Energy and Deciding to Live

The Dad:
The Missing Piece

WAIT, WHAT? Cinderella's dad doesn't even appear in the story, so why does he get a chapter? The thing is, I think the fact that the guy is not present in the story is a pretty important thing and affects Cinderella big time, and not just that she then gets physically stuck with a difficult step mum and sisters, but mentally lost too. He may not have the longest chapter, but he does have a role to play.

Let's look at what a father figure represents. Many people don't have a great father figure to go by, but we will look at what the father figure energy represents within us rather than any physical examples who are lost themselves. A father is that male energy of strength, power and support. In a perfect world, a father is someone you go to for sage advice, which supports your hopes and dreams and is a rock in life that you can trust to see you through any shit thrown your way in life. Father energy teaches us how to live openly, how to be courageous and fair, safe to live by our own values and our purpose. Even though we don't meet him in *Cinderella*, we know he was a rich businessman who married again to replace his daughter's mother. This seems to infer that his father energy was more directed to work than his daughter, although I can only make assumptions there because a). we don't have the facts or back story, and b). because it is actually a made-up fairy-tale fuckwittery

But that is how I choose to see this, so go with it. Without that father energy in her life, Cinderella has no one to go to for advice, no one to teach her how to be brave in life or have goals and what to do to get them. She has no real structure as that is a big part of father energy, straight-talking boundaries and structure. No wonder the poor cow floats around accepting everything life throws at her, simply dreaming of a night off and a posh frock, ready to give herself to the first person who shows any interest in her.

We need both male and female energy to be fully rounded, kick-arse humans. These energies are nothing to do with gender but what those different energies represent and do. Female energy is all about creating and nurturing, not necessarily in a mothering role, but creating all things. Female energy is a bit wild and free, which is all part of that creativity and gives birth to ideas and concepts. Female energy comes up with book plots, building design concepts, ideas for a theme park ride... any thoughts and ideas on creating things. Male energy then goes about the 'doing' part, how to execute those ideas into reality, works out what is needed and does it. We need to embrace both of those energies to achieve things in life. Stay centred in the female energy, and you will dream all your life without ever putting in any action to reach those dreams. Stay in male energy, and you will attempt to fix everything around you despite the fact they either do not need to be fixed or are unfixable.

With no idea or goal in mind, your masculine (taking action) energy gets lost in 'doing' with no positive result.

Stuck in the Creatives

I used to be stuck in female energy. I lived by my emotions and was incredibly creative. Oh, the ideas I came up with! Apart from drawing and painting, I came up with business after business ideas. Opening a Montessori school in my front room (that one never materialised, just stayed on paper), starting a singles social club (that one materialised briefly as Mad Jacks. I even got a dozen or so people paying £10 a month membership. I would visit possible venues and enjoy being shown around potential venues by sales guys and treated like a real businessperson. I created a few events, then it fizzled out), Celebratory Artist, which involved workshops in schools and community centres teaching people to make costumes or lanterns for carnivals and processions. This one became Darndog Arts, an arts company that also did other community art projects, but, just like the other ideas, it fizzled away to nothing.

I also tried setting up a dog walking service, a woman and a van service, art workshops for kids, illustrating, silver fingerprint jewellery (that one even had the idea of offering to take fingerprints from deceased loved ones!), making jewellery... the list goes on.

Friends and family were so enthusiastic at first, then dwindled down to a forced 'yay for you' sort of thing as my next idea would be presented, and then the next, and the next. Then they just didn't react at all. They had seen it all before and knew it would go nowhere. I was totally unaware of the idea of each of us having female and male energies and lived solely in my female creative side. Once I learned of the two and engaged my male energy into putting the actual work needed to make my ideas happen effectively, then my world changed. This book is one of the results for a start. I was now a trained and certified NLP coach and hypnotherapist and drew on many years of experience in mentoring and writing about what I knew and practised every day. My female energy had the idea to train in what I enjoyed, and my male side had put in the work and the knowledge. This time I did several drafts, going back and tweaking, changing and sorting. I sourced an editor, designer and proofreader. My male energy made my idea a reality rather than a half-arsed idea executed in a half-arsed way.

I want to be clear that when talking about male and female energies, I am not talking about alpha male or feminine goddess bollocks. Seriously, if you Google male energy, you get absolute guff about how to be more manly and attract women. Female energy searches will get you nonsense on attracting love with your feminine allure. All fucking stupid as you just need to start liking yourself and being your true, authentic self to attract the right people. Just ask RuPaul; he says, 'If you can't love yourself, how in the hell are you gonna love somebody else?' Reminding us that self-love is everything. What I am talking about is the different parts of you, your traits and ways of thinking. Cinderella is missing this energy and way of thinking, and it is represented by her absent father. The energy we draw on when it comes to *doing* rather than just thinking and dreaming, we need that father energy to be present in ourselves if we want to not just emotionally create our dreams and goals, but to put in the work needed to achieve it.

Decide, Decide, Decide

OK, Jools, that is easy to say, but how do I just draw up some do-it energy? Decide to. That's it. Deciding to put the work needed into your life changes everything. You already know my position on wishes and dreams; they get you nowhere. But the moment you decide, *really* decide, to act is when you find that inner father energy. It is there; it has always been there. It's just sometimes it gets so overwhelmed and hidden by our anxieties and insecurities that we forget it exists. Sometimes we were never told that we had it through those around us as we grew up not showing theirs or being toxic when showing our own father energy. But it is there, deep inside you, and you just need to believe. You need to be like Tinkerbelle in *Peter Pan*:

Believing in your own power and ability brings it back to life.

For Tinkerbelle, people not believing in her made her fade away, and it was only everyone shouting, 'I do believe in fairies, I do believe in fairies!' that she not only comes back but comes back stronger and more kick-arse than before. So, it's time to start shouting, 'I do believe in me, I do believe in me!' and start believing you have all the different parts and energies needed to become stronger and more kick-arse than ever. Decide to be all you need to be. Decide you believe in your own judgement, your own strength and your own self-worth. Decide to live.

Overview and Action Plan

- Recognise and accept the male and female energies within you that make you whole.
- Decide to believe in yourself, and you have all you need.
- Decide you can do this, and you have the strength.
- Decide to live.

Afformations

- How do I find it so easy to trust my judgement and decisions?
- Why do I believe in my own strength so easily?
- What do I need to do to be the best that I can be?

Journal Prompts

- What does my father energy want to tell me about my situation?
- What energy have I spent most of my life in?
- What do I need to acknowledge about this?

Chapter Nine

Taking Control of What You Can and Letting Go of the Rest

The King:
Ruling Your Kingdom

THE KING ONLY HAS A BIT PART in this story, or so it feels. Yet, he is the ruler of the kingdom. He is da boss! He watches over everything that happens and says yay or nay. In wanting the prince to get married, his prime motivation is for his own genes to carry on. For the prince to find someone to procreate with, so the bloodline continues. This is the ultimate motivation for all living things, to reproduce, and for people, that means not just yourself reproducing, but your offspring too, spreading yourself far and wide through your mini-me's. In the animal kingdom, some males kill any young they find that may not be theirs, but luckily, we as people don't go for that sort of thing, however much some people's kids seriously get on your tits.

Thus, the king wants his boy to get wed, get laid and make with the babies. As he is king, he sees nothing wrong in wanting it to happen right now, asap, this weekend at a push. The issue in hand takes all his time and energy, the idea that the prince must get married and produce heirs his sole thought rather than the right steps to take for the best outcome. Little things such as finding out what the prince himself would like or what sort of partner would suit him doesn't come into it for the king. Hell, he even assumes his son's gender preference. Keeping his kingdom safe and the continuation of his lineage is all the king can think about. He doesn't have time to sit and consider whether the issue at hand needs to be sorted or, indeed, can be sorted. It doesn't occur to the king that some things just, well, *are* and can be left alone.

Ruler of All You Survey

The king makes an excellent metaphor for the subconscious, which oversees our minds and bodies as a monarch would their lands. Never mind your body being a temple; it is a fucking kingdom, baby, yeah! The subconscious is constantly scanning for messages from its outposts for signals that anything is amiss. Intruders such as viruses or bacteria, correct hormone levels, oxygen levels, energy reserves etc... and of course, bear sightings. Remember that the brain is a bit over the top about bears, and seeing even the most minor issue as a potential man-eating bear which it will set off every alarm for, even if it was just a grumpy cat across the street? (See Chapter 2, pages 24-25.) I showed you how these alerts often come up due to old, false, negative beliefs, yet some alerts come from outside the kingdom walls, from the outside world.

We all have a wide range of concerns and worries –health, family, world issues, pandemics, risk of war and more, all looking like pretty big bloody bears. We have no control over these sorts of things, yet it's easy to focus a lot of time and energy worrying about them rather than spending that time and energy on things we *do* have control of or can do something about.

Stephen Covey came up with a fabulous way of looking at all this in his book *The 7 Habits of Highly Successful People* and calls it 'circle of concern/circle of influence'.[7] For our purpose, I'd like to present circles of control. The idea is to separate all your concerns into 'shit you can't control' and 'shit you can control', with a bit of 'shit you may not be able to control but can have some influence over' too. To have a balanced, kick-arse life, you need to turn off all the false bear alarms going off about shit you can do nothing about. Otherwise, said shit takes up so much time and energy that you have none left for shit you really should be concentrating on and doing something about. The king can spend too much time using his soldiers to bark at dragons and shout at clouds. So much so that they become a big part of life in the kingdom, everything is on permanent high alert, and the anxiety department is at full pelt. Now, if the king realised that he had no control over the existence of dragons or clouds and instead directed his soldiers to look at how they could protect themselves from rain and dragon shit (which must be enormous), the anxiety department could all take a tea break. Maybe even have the odd chocolate Hobnob as they calm down. He could then set up three separate new departments, new divisions and give the right time and energy each department deserve:

• Shit we know exists but can do nothing about it.
• Shit we can have and can't stop happening but can influence how it affects us.
• Shit we have we can do something about.

7 Covey, S. (1999). The 7 Habits of Highly Effective People. New York: Simon & Schuster.

That last department would get the biggest share of time and energy as it gives the best return on the goal of a fabulous, glitter-covered incredible life. The second department would get a pretty good share as it would provide us with answers to problems, new ideas on how to deal with stuff, protection etc., This means the first department can be an empty room as we learn to let that shit go. We can then direct our valuable resources, time and energy toward the last two departments, which can help us live better lives.

When to Give a Fuck and When to Give None

When I first became a single mum, my bear alerts were screaming. This was new territory, and I had no previous experience for my subconscious to draw upon, so it went into anxiety overdrive. When I had married, I went from living with my dad to living with a husband. There had been no in-between bit where I had a hip, chic pad and lived on my own or with other hip chicks. I wish I had, but you know how I feel about wishes, and regret is a pointless exercise, so the fact was that taking on full responsibility for myself, never mind for a small child, was completely new. There were six months where I went to college and stayed in digs at 17, but it didn't end well with me getting thrown out of college and being in debt, so it is possible that my subconscious took one look at that memory and was all 'We're fucked!'

The thing is, coming out of a bad marriage and having to be independent and responsible for both my daughter and me was the best thing that could have happened to me. It wasn't overnight teaching. It took a while for me to learn and grow but learn and grow I certainly did. Things I had considered beyond me and out of my control became either completely doable or things I could at least adjust to. I couldn't stop the bills coming in, but I could get rid of some and cut down on others. I couldn't stop my daughter from outgrowing clothes and shoes, but I could sort out contributions from her dad. At the time, I only had a limited amount of money coming in. Still, I had influence and control over what we could do for fun, and I became the master of cheap or free entertainment. One of our favourite trips was to IKEA. We would mess about in the room settings, getting into the beds and pretending to be cross at people coming into our rooms. Then we'd head off to the restaurant for cheap but yummy Swedish meatballs before heading out to the retail centre car park to sit in the car with an ice cream and watch the free show that was the gangs of young people obsessed with doing up their cars then showing them off. Who needed a zoo when you have the local RSPCA animal pound to wander around? Also, we lived not too far from Gatwick Airport, and my daughter loved the monorail that went between the terminals, so we would take a picnic, ride the monorail for a while and then go watch the aeroplanes taking off and landing. All free or cheap.

I may not have had any control over being a single mum, but I learned over time that I had control in more areas of my life than I realised. And if there were certain areas where I didn't have complete control, I at least had some influence, either in how I responded or dealing with things more positively rather than holding up my hands in total despair. I wish I had known about the circle of control exercise back then; I think

I would have worked it all out much quicker and stopped the anxiety right from the start, but I didn't, so I took the longer, harder route. Go through the exercise to discover where you could spend more time and energy and where to stop giving fucks.

Seriously, giving a fuck about something takes away from your internal bank account of time and energy, so make sure the things you do use those fucks on are a good return on your investment, even building up your reserves by filling you with positive energy and freeing up your time reserves for the fun stuff.

Exercise
Circle of Control

An easy way to work through your circles of control is to take a pad of sticky notes. On each one, write down a concern or worry. Get it all out and really brain dump them all. Then, with them spread out on the wall, start moving them around into three separate groups, under the following headings:

1. Shit we know exists but can do nothing about it.
2. Shit we can have can't stop happening but can have some influence over how it affects us.
3. Shit we have we can do something about.

Now take one of the worries or concerns and think about which group it can go in. Is it really something you have no control over whatsoever? If it is something like ill-health, then yes, you have no control over its existence or how other people act when it comes to it. But you can influence how *you* respond to it, such as eating well, having regular check-ups and maintaining a healthy body weight. You do not have total control over whether a disease will affect you or not, but you sure can do a bit to help yourself, so the disease could go in the 'some influence' group.

In the 'in my control' group, add:

• How I think.

• How I talk.

• How I act and react.

How you think, talk, act and react are all completely within your control and adding them to your list is a great visual reminder to work on these. How other people think, talk and act is not, but you may be able to influence the situation. Could you distance yourself from them? Vote for someone with values nearer to yours? Go to family therapy sessions or mediation? Look for compromise? Maybe go through the three-chair position exercise from earlier and see if you can spot their side? (See Chapter 4, page 73.)

Then there is the 'shit I can do nothing about' group, which could be things like traffic, wars, the economy or having to go to work (or is this something you have some influence over, such as where and what you do for that work). You have no control over this stuff whatsoever, so this is the group you need to let go of to not waste your precious time and energy on. In giving any real focus on these sorts of issues, they take away from where your focus could actually help. We all know people who are so wrapped up in being anxious about current affairs or in full panic mode about diseases and pandemics that not only do those things take up their very existence, but their bear alerts are screaming so loud that their anxiety levels are through the roof. Maybe one of the sticky notes for the 'shit totally in my control' needs to read 'Things I choose to worry about'. Because what you worry about really is up to you.

What I find when I go through this exercise with clients is that the 'no control' list gets smaller and smaller as they start to realise they have at least some small influence on many things, if not total control, and so the 'some influence' group that gets bigger and bigger. When you have worked on it for a bit, taking your time and digging deep, you could fill out the diagram of the circles to have a more permanent reminder. Always make sure your two positive circles take up the most significant amount of your life; they are the ones that will make your life soar!

Overview and Action Plan

- Your king/subconscious is always on the lookout for bears and can become fixated on focussing on the stuff you have no control over.
- Your anxiety levels can become constantly raised if you focus on things you can't control or influence rather than things you can do something about.
- Give your time and energy to the stuff that will create a better life and decrease your stress and anxiety.

Afformations

- Why do I find it so easy to let go of worries and concerns that I have no control over and act on those things I do have control or influence over?
- What do I need to do to believe in my own abilities?

Journal Prompts

- What is my biggest worry right now?
- What actions can I take today to help myself?
- What do I need to let go of right now?

Chapter Ten

Speaking to Yourself with Compassion and Love

The Queen:
Owning Your Crown

THE QUEEN DOESN'T MUCH COME INTO THE STORY at all, so it appears at first. Her role is the other half to the king, the yin to his yang, the fish to his chips, the Minnie to his Mickey, the tea to his biscuit. He may reign over the kingdom, but she is there by his side –the voice of reason, that part that he trusts and loves. The queen is your own voice of reason, your self-talk, which we all do and is entirely natural, healthy and a sign of an intelligent mind, not the first sign of madness as you were probably told. However, using the right words can change everything, making the king lookout for his kingdom in the most fabulous, life-changing way.

How Do You Self-talk?

Self-talk starts early, with toddlers doing it out loud. When they are engrossed in play or a task, they often talk out loud to themselves as they go. They could be playing with their toy cars when you hear them say, 'This car is dirty, I need to wash it, I need water – Mum, can I have some water? I want to wash all my cars and then put them in my bed to dry.' Part of that self-talk was to mum, but most of it was talking aloud as they identified the problem and what could be done about it. The answers they come up with may not appear rational, but this is a toddler brain talking to itself. When, as a mum, you come across a bed full of wet cars, your adult brain is all what the hell? But to a brain that has only been around a couple of years, it makes complete sense as that is where they go after a bath.

As children mature, that self-talk becomes internalised and becomes what we all do, our inner chatter. It starts to be a bit shit and limits us when that self-talk is negative. Imagine how the king in Cinderella would be if all day, every day he heard, 'What the hell are you doing? You know people will realise you are a total imposter and can't do this, don't you? You are so bloody fat. No one will love you. God, you are clumsy; it's so embarrassing. I wouldn't even bother trying. You'll only end up looking an idiot.' This type of self-talk 24/7 would leave him like a puddle on the floor, unable to get out of bed, never mind take care of the kingdom and sort out dragons.

What we say to ourselves matters, so how the actual flip can we stop destroying our chances at living our best lives with negative self-talk? Simple, swap it for positive self-talk. OK, so the concept isn't rocket science but, getting into the habit of speaking nicely to yourself, using positive words and being your own cheerleader makes life so much more fucking awesome.

Sweet Talking Self-love

First, embrace positive language. Learn to use it, love it and smooch the arse off it. We often feel an instant wall go up when it comes to complimenting ourselves or bigging ourselves up. When someone you've just met asks what you do, is your usual answer simply your job title, said in an almost apologetic tone? Have you ever said instead, 'Oh,

I'm a ... and am damn great at it! I jump out of bed every morning with excitement over it!'? OK, you may have a job you hate (so get another one already), but you know what I mean, have you ever bigged yourself up when talking to someone else? Do you get awkward and embarrassed when someone else gives you a compliment? Time to start practising with some positive language. Not crazy sort of self-talk, just talking kindly and with compassion to yourself.

Don't get me wrong, there will be times when it will be damn hard; some situations just aren't positive. You probably won't be at Aunt Agatha's funeral saying, 'Yes, it's terribly sad, but I did a great eulogy, didn't I? Not a dry eye in the house, I was brilliant.' But in general, in day-to-day life, start spotting when you put yourself down, even jokingly and stop yourself. Then practise putting in the odd positive word or two or tell people things you are proud of. The more you practice, the more natural it will become.

Take a couple of little steps towards positive self-talk today and make them a daily habit. Small things build up, one by one. Think of one snowflake and an avalanche. Just start with a snowflake or two and see where it takes you.

Exercise
Using Affirmations

As discussed in Chapter 2, affirmations are positive self-talk that you often repeat to change how your subconscious mind responds. But if you are not truly feeling the statement, then just saying stuff like 'I love my body' can feel fake and stupid, so don't feel obliged to go overboard with the old positivity. Saying 'I am learning to love my body' will ring truer and be more believable deep down inside. Practise what works for you, not what some printed happy affirmation sticker says (unless you spotted it because it totally resonated, and yes, little bundle of fluffy kitty, you WILL hang in there!).

Overview and Action Plan

- Your queen/inner self-talk can build you up or incapacitate you – it is your doing, your choice.
- It is natural to talk to yourself; just watch how you do it.
- Anxiety levels can become constantly raised if you tune into your negative self-talk.
- Give your time and energy to the stuff that will create a better life and decrease stress and anxiety.

Afformations

- Why do I find it so easy to let go of worries and concerns that I have no control over and take action on those things I do have control or influence over?
- What do I need to do to believe in my own abilities?

Journal Prompts

- Where do I talk negatively to myself the most? Can I spot a common theme?
- My strengths and positive qualities include [*list as many as you can*]:
- Write a letter to your five-year-old self describing their strengths and positive characteristics.

Chapter Eleven

Finding Your Ikigai, Your Purpose

Your Happy Ever After

NOW TO FIND YOUR HAPPY-EVER-AFTER, and you can find it all by yourself, you don't need to wait for some foot-obsessed dude to come banging on your door or for some weirdo who thinks you are lying dead in the woods to come and kiss you. You've got this all by yourself. If you have gone through each chapter so far and worked through the exercises, you are in the best place for your happy ending, especially in knowing your core values in life and who you really are.

I said at the beginning of this book how I always felt frustrated when a fairy story simply finished with 'And they lived happily ever after.' How even as a child, I felt hard done by, left without the most critical part of the story, *how* they lived happily ever after. What did they do to be happy for the next six decades? (Maybe even seven or eight decades as most fairy-tale princesses seemed to have just turned 16 in the stories.) Was it easy? Was there a secret I should know?

Hide and Seek Happiness

When I looked around my own world, I couldn't see anyone living 'happily ever after'. Adults seemed to be either slogging their guts out doing a job they moaned about or spent their days doing household chores – cleaning the toilet, doing the laundry. None of that looked like it could be the definition of a happy ever after, so what did the folks in the story do? Was just being in love the thing? Again, as I looked around at adults in my world, that didn't seem to be it either. I saw even the best of couples fed up with other areas of their life, or I saw people living on their own who seemed happy as Larry, so that didn't fit. What the actual fuck were these books trying to pull?

As a youngster, I fell in love often. Whether it was Captain Scarlett, Donny Osmond, Les from The Bay City Rollers or even a new toy. I can still pull up the feelings of complete joy at the ventriloquist doll I had one Christmas or my Ballerina Sindy doll with bendy legs in teeny weeny tights that I would bend into gruesome poses forwards and sideways. (Dear God, I hope she wasn't linked to anyone like some creepy voodoo doll.) That buzz in your belly from either a crush or in owning something longed for. It was the 'happy' part, but the 'ever after' bit never really materialised. Les from The Bay City Rollers came after my devotion to Donny had lost its edge. After Les came the boy in my year at school. At the time, all these were true loves as far as I was concerned. Thank fuck I didn't instantly marry any of them like fairy-tale girls seem to do. Same as when I set my heart on a new toy or even a beret. I was so sure that life from the point of ownership would be bloody amazing, that I would be happy forevermore. And I was happy, for however long it took to be bored of that thing and set my sights on a new thing, because that new thing was now definitely it, my happy ever after.

Now, in my 50s, I have finally found the secret to having your happy-ever-after, and the most frustrating part is that it was never a secret in the first place. The Japanese had understood what it was for centuries, and it was just us westerners who were farting about trying to find it and not simply asking if anyone had sussed it. Those fabulous Japanese knew it all along and would have shared if we had ever thought to mention it. They had something they called ikigai.

The first thing about happy-ever-after is the word happy. What does that word actually mean? I looked up the *Oxford English Dictionary* definition of happiness, which is simply 'The state of being happy.' OK, that's a start, if not a bit basic. I looked up happy, 'feeling or showing pleasure or contentment.' It seemed to be saying happiness is a state or condition in the *present* tense, which kind of infers it can be fleeting and maybe not precisely the 'ever after' we are looking for.

In psychology, happiness is often abbreviated to SWB, standing for subjective wellbeing, and the critical word there is *subjective*, meaning it can be different for everyone. A beautiful rosy newborn baby will make the parents and grandparents deliriously happy, but office colleagues less so when they have to sit through 12,184 photos of a blob that looks like every other snotty red-faced baby out there. Much to my own amazement Captain Scarlet didn't make others happy in the same way he made me happy, with his rugged good looks and, literally, chiselled jaw. So, happiness is different for each of us and tends to be in the present, a feeling that will not be constant but nice enough at the time.

Comfy and Cosy Happiness

The Danish have something they call *Hygge* (pronounced 'hooga' and not higgy, as I called it for some time) which translates as 'celebrating every day'. Hygge is all about that feeling of a lovely atmosphere, all hot chocolate and big, oversized knitted blankets in front of a log fire, or the cosy feeling of a games night with friends and drinks. Still lovely and happy, but again, not 'ever after'. It would make me happy at the time, and sure, I guess you could put it in the diary to do into the future, but it still doesn't feel 'ever-after to me, plus all that hot chocolate and lazing around and my gut would need several of those cosy blankets just to cover it.

So *Hygge* is nice and probably important to have as *part* of your life. Yet it is a present tense thing again, happiness but not necessarily something that would make me jump out of bed every morning. The Swedish have a similar thing that they call *mysig*, so maybe living somewhere cold increases a need for needing to feel cosy and snuggly. The Swedes also have the word *lagam*, which means not too little, not too much and is all about decluttering and having balance in your life, which sounds nice and maybe something to add to life in general. I think it all rather excellent, and I high-five the Swedes and Danes on it all, a pinch of *lagam* with a big dash of *Hygge* hot chocolate, and you may be on the way to a pretty nice ever after.

But something for me still felt it was missing. Then I discovered the Japanese concept of *ikigai* and realised these guys had nailed happy-ever-after. Japan has some of the oldest people globally, and *ikigai* is probably a big part of the reason as it helps them continue to find meaning in their lives long into old age. They had a purpose in their lives which made them healthier, motivated and happy... ever after!

Pronounced eee-keeeey-guy, not eye-key-guy and definitely not icky-guy. The difference is being happy every day for the rest of your life versus that overly tanned 90-year-old letchy guy on the beach in leopard print Speedos and not something you want to get the wrong way round. Say it as if grinning the whole way through. The word *ikigai* is formed from two words, *iki* meaning alive or life, and *gai,* meaning benefit or worth. Put together, *ikigai* means your life worth or life purpose; it is what makes you jump out of bed in the morning, every morning... a *really* happy-ever-after.

One thing the Japanese don't have a word for is retirement as we know it, as in stopping employed-work life and relaxing. They don't see the end of your employment life as any sort of end at all; it is merely a transition into different work. This can be any work or activities that make you happy and wake up in the morning knowing you will be rocking your thing again, your *ikigai*. Your *ikigai* isn't something only to start when you get older and stop work either. Discovering yours will make your life happier at any stage and more kick-arse and knowing it will lead you through to the very end with a smile on your face.

Anyone Seen My Purpose?

I wish I had learned about *ikigai* in my youth. I have always felt a little bit lost, separate from the rest of the world and almost alien to it. As I looked around, it felt as if everyone else was getting on in life, having great careers which they loved, nice houses, fancy cars and unforgettable holidays, etc. Yeah, I realise that it is a small proportion of people in the world living this seemingly wonderful life, but they were the people I focussed on when I was wondering what the hell my 'thing' was. I felt deep in my gut that something was missing; I had no purpose. As I described in Chapter 00, from my 20s, I started business after business trying to find that purpose; creative workshops, a singles membership club, illustration, portrait artist, dog portrait artist, dog walker, art coach...and that's just naming a few! I was sure that when the right idea hit, my purpose would show itself, my 'thing' would jump up and shout, 'Here I am! Your thing! Your purpose! From now on, life is gonna be sweeeeet! But that never happened.

I knew vaguely what made me happy. I loved being creative, especially painting, which took me to that 'other place' where you are unaware of anything around you, including time – which I now know is called being in a state of *flow*. I also realise now that working for someone else was not a part of who I am as I constantly started self-employed business after self-employed business, clearly preferring to be an entrepreneur somehow, some way. I didn't use the word entrepreneur. I just had this unwavering need to do something myself that people would like enough to pay me for. Whenever I did try and work for someone, it would be in shops as I loved interacting with customers. It didn't dawn on me that interacting with people was part of my joys in life, not on a conscious level. I just knew I was good with people, and jobs in shops were always a go-to thing.

Seriously, all the clues were there if I had only known how to go about it all! I also loved working with kids, so I worked as a teaching assistant in several schools. I was always put with kids who had behavioural issues because it became very apparent that I worked well with them, probably because I had been one of them myself. I never 'talked down' to kids, I spoke to them with respect as I would an adult but on a knowledge level that fitted each one personally, and they recognised that. Kids can spot a fake grown-up at 10 paces, and they instantly recognise a truthful one, which means trust and rapport, although not necessarily instant, sure came quicker.

I remembered how I hated school from the day I started aged four to the day I left at 16. I felt like I was in an alien world and understood nothing. I kind of was, in a way, as I now know I am dyspraxic, which is in the dyslexic family but has body control issues thrown in for good measure. I was always falling over my own feet! I went back to visit my primary school in my 30s, and the now ageing receptionist immediately said, "Julia Teare! Are you still falling over?" For fuck's sake, no 'how are you, what have you done with your life, are you happy?' Nope, all she remembered was that I constantly fell arse over tit and bled all over her office. I suppose you would remember someone like that.

I was always last to be picked for sports teams due to my poor body control too, and I dreaded sports day, which, as far as I was concerned, should have been renamed public humiliation day. My dyspraxic brain had trouble taking in many points at once. Concepts and ideas I can do, but having facts dictated from the front of the classroom did not work for me, and I felt stupid for it. Anyway, remembering how school was something that I just did not understand, how

I was made to feel so dumb for not remembering my times' tables or keywords in physics or geography gave me empathy with these kids. I could explain concepts and lessons in words they understood. I recognised and understood their anger, their confusion as it had been mine, and they responded by identifying I was on their side and not the enemy.

Your Personal Genius

I had felt so stupid at school that, as an adult, I did a Mensa test to find out my actual level of stupidity. That sounds crazy, but I had also just come out of an abusive relationship and was repeatedly told I was stupid, so I decided to find out once and for all. Turns out I am far from it, at least as far as Mensa is concerned. My IQ is, in fact, quite high. Having dyspraxia, my brain wiring, made remembering things tricky, but my understanding of concepts was outstanding. The fact I had to work with this and learnt to explain what I meant or what I was talking about differently, in a more lateral way, gave me my genius, as in my unique ability, not the mind of Einstein.

I encourage you to learn to use the word genius and feel comfortable with it. Your genius is your thing, what you are good at, your skill. We all have one, whether we are green-fingered, great at football or being able to do perfect eyeliner wings. We shall come back to this later as it will be part of finding your *ikigai*.

So what did this have to do with finding my purpose, my *ikigai*? I now understand that explaining things in basic terms is part of what makes me happy. Sharing knowledge and information in a simple way that will improve life for others is part of my thing. I just needed to find the other parts, but it was slowly coming together, I was starting to see my thing, and life started to feel pretty damn good, but I felt there was more.

Throughout my childhood and adulthood, I always felt unheard and was often criticised for how I spoke. I can still hear my mum telling me, 'It's not jiiiine, it's jaaaaane, remember you are from Surrey!' whenever I called out to my cousin. Put all this together, and boy, did I doubt my own voice. Being heard is now one of my life joys. Not in a being loud and making neighbours cross sort of way, although I still catch myself worrying about that, just having people listen to what I have to say, hear my message... hear my truth. As for my accent, I have learned to love that I do not sound straight out of *Downton Abbey* but a bit more *Gimme*, it is who I really am, a touch more Linda La Hughes than Lady Mary. I have tried to sound a bit 'posher' in the past, thinking people would respect me more. Now I am proud that although I may come from Surrey, it is the very edge of Surrey, with the centre of Croydon just 5 miles or so away, and yes, I have an estuary accent. And do you know what? People respect me, despite that. What a revelation! So having my message heard in my authentic, from the soul's voice was part of my thing, part of my happiness.

Now that I have found the real me and discovered that I bloody love real Jools, I have found my *ikigai*, my 'thing' – helping others to believe in themselves again too. That purpose in life gets me up every morning buzzing with anticipation for the day to come. To share with the world how to be authentic, confident and love yourself again, THAT is my *ikigai*! Sure, I throw in a good measure of *Hygge* hot chocolate (with a shot of brandy, please), fun with friends and art just to make my life feel bloody lovely, but that is the thing with ikigai; it is *all* the good stuff that makes your heart sing. It's having all that good stuff that helps you cope better with any occasional bad shit that life can throw up, and mainly it creates your happy ever after, a *real* happy ever after, a life with meaning and purpose.

What Will My *Ikigai* Look Like?

Dan Buettner, American National Geographic Fellow and *New York Times* bestselling author, discovered the five places in the world, which he called 'Blue Zones',[8] where people live the longest, healthiest lives. These Blue Zones have many common factors, one of which is that the inhabitants have a strong sense of purpose. Sure, their diet and physical health come into it, but they have a deep, knicker-wetting belief in their life purpose. Seems that being happy to see a new day, to look forward to what that day will bring, keeps you going and going and going.

So, how do you go about finding yours? To start with, understand that it is not necessarily all about your work or career. I had assumed it was all about my career as I watched others around me knowing what they wanted to do as a job and then romping through the promotions and pay rises. Your *ikigai,* your purpose, can be work, but it can also be

8 Buettner, D. (2012) *The Blue Zones*. Washington DC: National Geographic.

a hobby or a person; it is whatever gives your life value and allows you to feel fulfilled. Maybe I had been a bit down on those fairy-tale dudes. Perhaps they really did get by on loving each other. Yeah, I'm still not convinced to be honest; I think having a good mix of work, hobby and people may work best. A big dollop of something you love doing and get money for, a dash of something you love doing because you are pretty good at it and it brings you pleasure as well as taking you to that 'other place' where you completely zone out, and a healthy splash of people, both personal people like lovers, friends and family as well as people in a community, either your neighbourhood community or a community of like-minded crazies that also love *Dungeons and Dragons* or hugging trees (I do love a tree hug).

Snow White seemed happiest with her seven little guys or doing the housework with the local wildlife whilst belting out a solid tune. I may not get any help with the dusting from my cat or the local crows, but I do love to belt one out; the funkier, the better, while I prance about with the vacuum. I am not saying that housework is my *ikigai*, no fucking way, and my husband will be nodding furiously in agreement that it is not a joy to me, but a tidy house is a joy to me. A neat house calms my mind and makes me feel damn good, so if I am doing it, it is for the outcome of a congenial environment rather than because it is a chore that needs doing. Sometimes that is a part of *ikigai*, doing even the little things with pleasure as the core reason. If you want a tidy house, make the business end fun by howling along to Abba (one of my housework faves) and shaking your booty. And if you can get the odd wildlife or two to do a bit of dusting to help you out whilst also adding backing singing to your rendition of Mamma Mia, then you are kicking butt!

Why have I suddenly started on about cleaning as part of your happy ever after? Are you now shouting, 'That's it? Housework will make me jump out of bed every morning jumping for joy? What the buggering buggery!'? Dear God, no, it was that Snow White dude that got me on to that. I am saying that happy ever after isn't down to one big thing; it is all the little things too. It is feeling good in your body for one thing. It is no good living to a ripe old age, yet being so unfit and unhealthy, you can do nothing but lay on the sofa and watch the rest of the world living it large. It is about appreciating all the little things as well as the big life goals and achievements – those little things that have meaning for you.

I love stopping at little cafes with outside tables, having a coffee and watching the world go by. That is a small thing, but to me, it is also a big thing as I enjoy it so much. I enjoy being by myself, lost in thought as I people watch, or if I am more honest, dog watch. I am smiling as I write about my cafe moments as my subconscious remembers those moments, and I feel the same sense of pleasure and contentment as when I am physically there.

The brain is good at that sort of thing, bringing up the feelings remembered from a past experience. This can be shit if you bring up bad memories. But if you train yourself – make a habit of remembering the good stuff, of deliberately sitting for a few minutes and thinking about a kick-arse time you had, really focussing on all the details like what you could see, hear, smell – then you can bring up all the positive, nice feelings you had then and feel them again, right now. If you then fill your days enjoying the little things, finding the good in the dullest of things, such as singing as you clear up, your brain will learn that happiness is the default setting.

Finding your happiness default setting doesn't mean that shit will no longer happen in life. Life is what it is, and it will always throw things our way, but you will ride that stuff so much better.

Exercise
Finding Your *Ikigai*

Okay, so let's get you finding your *ikigai.* A popular image for finding your purpose or calling is a four circle Venn diagram, showing how the four components of what makes up your true purpose overlap, with your ikigai revealing itself in the centre due to being in all four circles. The four areas are

• What you love.
• What you are good at.
• What the world needs.
• What you could be rewarded or paid for.

In finding which answer fits all four areas, you find your purpose, your thing, your *ikigai.*

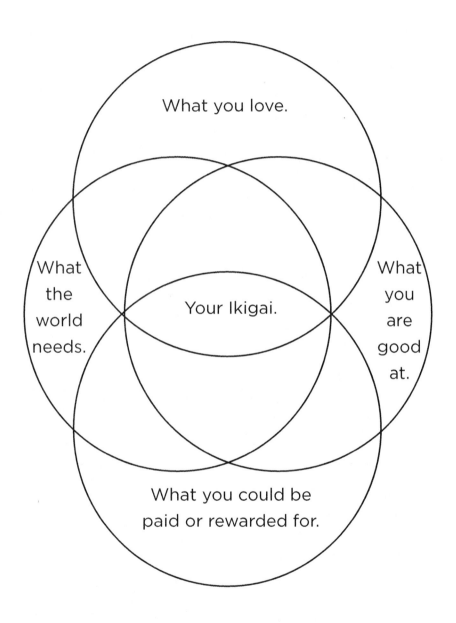

What you love.

What the world needs.

Your Ikigai.

What you are good at.

What you could be paid or rewarded for.

There are some questions to go through for each of those four areas so you can find the answers true to you, so you will need either your journal or some paper, and most importantly, some time and space to do some soul searching.

What do you love?

• What did you love doing or thinking about as a child?

• What are your passions or hobbies?

• What takes you to 'that other place'/zone (known as flow)?

• What are you known for liking by others?

What you are good at?

• What are your skills?

• What do others say you are good at?

• What do friends/family/work colleagues come to you for advice or help with?

• What do you find easy that others don't?

What does the world need?

• What inspires you in the world and gets your juices up and why?

• Who inspires you and why?

• What annoys you in the world and why?

• Who annoys you and why?

• What could you be paid or rewarded for?

• What thing or service could be exchanged for a reward?

• What job do you feel would totally suit you?

• What job do others say would totally suit you?

Answering these questions is not something to do in 10 minutes and say 'Ta-dah! Done it!' Although seeing what answers come to you quickly and easily will be interesting. Really explore each question, think about it over a few days, even weeks. Ask those around you what they think. Gradually a bigger and clearer picture will begin to emerge. Some of it you will have been very aware of, other things will more 'I didn't realise but can now totally see that' moments. I found asking people what they know me for or remember me as a child to be so enlightening, as well as what they thought my skills were.

When you have collected all the information and answers, either start highlighting ones that appear in more than one area or put them into a Venn diagram and see what pops up in the centre due to being in all four sections. This is your purpose, your *ikigai*.

It may take days or even months to find your purpose and then align yourself with it. Once you have identified your purpose, what will have you jumping out of bed in the morning, you will need time to work out how to put it into your life. Do you need to change jobs or just direction within your job? Would starting your own business be your thing? Do you now see what you need to add to your life or what was missing? This is where you can start putting everything into place to be living your *ikigai*. An important thing to remember also is that your purpose is not set in stone. Your purpose today may not be your purpose next year or in ten years, and that is okay. It is *all* okay.

*This is YOUR life to live your way.
No apologies, no excuses, no guilt.
Write your own story
and create the life you want to live*

Overview and Action Plan

- Happiness is appreciating all the little things.
- Knowing your purpose/your thing and aligning your life around it will keep you jumping out of bed in the morning happily ever after.
- Your *ikigai* is organic and may change as time goes by.
- It is ALL OK. You, your needs, your likes, your life.

Afformations

- What do I need to do to be true to myself?
- Why do I find it so easy to live life with purpose?
- How do I always know exactly what I need to do to be happy?

Journal Prompts

- Where in my life am I working against my purpose?
- What do I need to give myself permission to change in my life?
- Where can I start creating little personal happiness habits or actions today?
- What steps can I put in place to start aligning my life to my purpose?

Final Words

The End and the Start

A GOOD WHILE BACK, one of my most liked photos ever was in a Facebook group, and I put on my introduction post. I have very little makeup on, messy hair and have my hands on my hips with my tongue defiantly stuck out. I was also wearing a tee-shirt with cartoon boobs on the front (it was for a breast cancer charity). For all the past photos in my online life where I had carefully posed and filtered to within an inch of my life, it was this spontaneous, natural shot that caught people's attention. It was me being the real, authentic person I am deep in my soul. I wasn't trying to impress anyone, I wasn't trying to conform to society's definition of what constitutes beauty or sexiness, and I wasn't trying to be anything I wasn't really. It was raw, authentic Jools and strangers across the world hit their like buttons. Many commented with things like 'I wish I could do a great photo like that' – which made me sad. Why couldn't they? What was stopping them from feeling carefree and confident in themselves that meant a natural photo displayed to the world was out of the question? Who told them it was out of the question? Whose story were they living?

I believe that deep down, we all have queen energy, that sense of self-worth, self-confidence, knowing want we want from life and taking it! But sometimes life knocks us off course or floors us altogether, and that inner queen gets lost, and we need to start over, to be reminded that we own a crown and choose our own path in life.

It is time to write your OWN story! This is YOUR life, and it is time to start living it your way. You get to be the lead, to decide the plot and who gets supporting roles and who gets cut completely. If those capital letters look shouty, then good because I want to shout it. Be loud, be proud and go live your life your way, with the hap-hap-happiest ever after.

The end.

Your new beginning.

About the Author

 Originally from Surrey, having lived in Oxford and next to the sea in Fife, Jools now resides in the North Staffordshire Moorlands with her Scottish husband and a cat called Minge, where she drinks far too much tea yet is the happiest she has ever been. She does miss the sea, though.

Jools Riddell is a certified NLP coach, clinical hypnotherapist, course creator, personal cheerleader, motivational ass-kicker, lover of tea and straight talk, and author. Her mission is to help women across the globe to start over and change their life stories, remember who they are, find their lost spark and start building a life that excites them.

Acknowledgements

Thanks to everyone who surrounded with me with love, support, and huge doses of patience as I wrote this book. My beloved father, or Aged P as he is lovingly known, who has always had me believe in the hidden magic in the world and ourselves. Debra Jones, who has been my personal cheerleader from the idea through to the finished book and who kicks my butt. She is my rock and one of the most ridiculously awesome humans on this planet. Huge thanks and slurpy wet kisses to my support troop: Susie and Howard, Hannah, Jax and all the rest. To Minge the cat for her company and sitting on important piles of paper for me. Also my patient and wonderful editor Sandy Draper and my design wonder that is Catherine Murray.

Printed in Great Britain
by Amazon

71921716R00108